MILLIONAIRE
BARBER STYLIST
How to Retire from Behind the Chair

The Millionaire Barber Stylist
published by:
(Uchendi Nwani) dba
International Barber & Style College
3744 Annex Avenue Suite A 2
Nashville, TN 37209
1-615-354-0166

Produced by True Vine Publishing Company
P.O. Box 22448, Nashville, TN. 37202
www.TrueVinePublishing.org

Copyright, 2013 by Uchendi Nwani. All rights reserved. No part of this book may be used or reproduced in any manner whatsoever without written permission. For information, please write to the address above.

For speaking engagements, books, dvds or workshops-

E-mail: 1chin@comcast.net
Web Site: www.millionairebarberstylist.com

THE MILLIONAIRE BARBER STYLIST
How to Retire from Behind the Chair

Velma Demonbreun
&
Unchendi Nwani

DEDICATION

This book is dedicated to my mentor, advisor and friend, Velma J. Demonbreun, who taught me everything about the hair industry and school business. Your knowledge and guidance kept me going and thousands of others across the nation. Every successful person has a mentor that has helped them reach their goals. I could not have achieved all of my goals without the help of Velma Demonbreun.

Velma Demonbreun started in this business to help other Barbers & Stylist achieve their dreams. You may have seen her on TV with Debye Tuner reporter from New York CBS 'The Early Show', or teaching Demetria Kalodimos how to do a manicure on channel 4 WSMV. The "Back Road Show' with Terry Bulger channel 4 WSMV and the "Talk Of The Town Show" channel 5 WTVF.

She has received many awards. She was Voted Who's Who, Woman of The Year, Business women of the year, Professional Women Award, Leader in Beauty Education, Dress for Success Award, The most likely to succeed Award and the Star Award in Education.

She has been in the hair industry for over 45 years, graduating thousands of barber and cosmetology students and helping them open their own barber and beauty salons, beauty and barber schools.

ACKNOWLEDGMENTS

The success of The Barber & Styling School has brought us many new friends from all over in the hair industry.

To the barber stylist with whom I've worked with to produce the ideas that are presented in this book. To Velma Demonbreun for giving me the answers and guidance in the hair industry.

FOREWORD

It has been over twenty years since I started in the hair industry. A lot has happened in the interim with my family, my business and my life. Many wonderful things, many good things, and many painful things. It is not important what happens to us in life, but it is important how we respond to what happens to us in life. It does not matter the cards we were dealt in life, it is how we play the cards we were dealt. If life gives you lemons, make some lemonade.

In my journey, I have experienced near financial and business disaster as well as incredible victories. My mentor (Velma Demonbreun) and I have created a rich and abundant school where we teach countless barber stylist what we have learned about running a barber styling school, opening a barber salon, about leadership, time management and about financial independence. All of this will awaken the spirit of entrepreneurship in you. We have spoken to thousands of barber stylist, salon owners and school owners throughout the United States and our work has been spread all over. Velma and I created the two day workshops to help you get from where you are to where you want to be.

This book answers many questions that Barber Stylist have raised over the years, offering them the opportunity to approach their business with renewed vigor and a sharpened mindset.

TABLE OF CONTENTS

Introduction:		13
Chapter 1:	The Millionaire Mindset	15
Chapter 2:	How to Achieve More by Working Less	18
Chapter 3:	Starting from the Bottom	27
Chapter 4:	A New Beginning	33
Chapter 5:	The Booth Rental/Commission Barber	39
Chapter 6:	The Entrepreneur, Manager & Barber	44
Chapter 7:	The Barber Stylist First Phase	51
Chapter 8:	Silver Phase: Getting Some Help	59
Chapter 9:	Beyond the Comfort Zone	65
Chapter 10:	Gold Phase: Entrepreneur Mindset	75
Chapter 11:	Turn Key Barber Styling Revolution	78
Chapter 12:	The Business Format	81
Chapter 13:	Barber Styling School Business Plan	87
Chapter 14:	Booth Rental Contract	103

Chapter 15: Things I Learned From My 131
Mentor

Chapter 16: Hot to Run a Million-Dollar 138
School

Seminar 144

INTRODUCTION

I think that maybe inside any barber styling business, someone is slowly going crazy. If you are a barber stylist, salon owner or school owner, this book was written for you. It represents thousands of hours of work we have done over twenty years. It illustrates the experiences we have had with the thousands of barber styling students, licensed barber stylist, salon owners and school owners with whom we've helped.

And what we have discovered is that the people who are in the hair industry work far more than they should for the return they're getting. The problem is not that the barber stylist does not work hard; the problem is that they're doing the work wrong and mismanaging money. As a result, most barber stylist end up stressed out, burned out, not growing, financially unstable and working behind the chair for life. The trade that they once loved, they began to dislike.

Barber Styling salons start and fail in the United States at an increasingly staggering rate. Every year thousands of barber stylist start a business. Statistics tell us by the end of the first year at least 45 percent of them will be out of business. Within five years, more than 70 percent of them will have failed. And the rest of the bad news is, if you are a barber stylist that has managed to survive for the five years or more, don't feel lucky. Because more than 85 percent barber stylist that have survived the first five years fail in the second five years, because they are only working behind the chair all day long and not having any time for themselves .

Why is this?

Why do so many barber stylist go into business, only to fail?

What are they not learning?

Why are some barber stylist and school owners rich and wealthy while others are broke and slaving behind the chair?

How do some school owners become accredited and receive financial aid while others struggle to stay open? Why is it that with all the information available today on how to be successful in the hair industry, so few barber stylist really are? This book answers those questions. It's about systems, information, networking, ideas, which, if you understand and use them, it will help you get from where you are to where you want to be. Ignore them, and you will likely join the thousands of barber stylist and school owners who pour their energy, money and time into the hair industry and fail, or the many others who struggle for years working behind the chair simply trying to survive.

My Reason for Becoming a School Owner
My primary reason for becoming a school owner was a desire to provide a better life, financial education, more time with my family and entrepreneurship. We wanted to make this information available to anyone who wanted to learn, regardless of how much money they had or where they were in life. That is why we started the barber styling school for students and our two day workshop for license barber stylist and school owners.

So, what exactly is the "How To Run A Million Dollar School Seminar"?

It is a 2 day live training program that shows you, step-by-step, how to build a unique and profitable Barber & Styling School, become accredited, receive government grants, market more effectively and turn your school into a 24/7 money-making, world-changing school. We're honored to have barber stylist from all over the United States experience this life changing workshop each week. Velma and I have over seventy years of combined experience in this industry.

CHAPTER 1

THE MILLIONAIRE BARBER STYLIST MINDSET

This book is written for barbers and stylist who are ready to change, especially for individuals who are currently working behind the chair and want to move beyond the chair and achieve financial security.

Early in my career, my mentor (Velma) told me a simple story that guided me to great joy and financial freedom. It was her way of explaining the difference between a rich barber stylist and a poor barber stylist. The story goes like this:

"Once upon a time there was this small town. It was a great place to live except for one problem. The town had no barber stylist unless your friend or family member performed the service in your kitchen. To solve this problem once and for all, the mayor asked many barber stylist to submit bids to perform hair care services to the people each day. Two people were awarded the contracts, so it would keep competition prices competitive and it would ensure everyone in the town had their hair serviced on a regular basis.

"The first person who won the contract, John, immediately ran out bought a barber styling kit and began working in the barber styling salon each day. He immediately began making money as he worked from early morning to late night each day. He would stand behind the chair over twelve hours each day cutting, fading, shaving, styling, shampooing, relaxing and coloring hair. He never had time to spend with his wife and children. Each morning he had to get up before the rest of the town awoke to make sure his barber styling tools and products were ready for the people. It was hard work, but he was happy to be making money and for having one of the two exclusive contracts for this hair business. The second winning barber stylist, Mary, disappeared for a while. She wasn't seen for months, which made John very happy, since he had no competition.

"Instead of buying a barber styling kit to compete with John, Mary wrote a business plan, created a corporation, found 2 investors, employed a manager to do the work, and returned six months later with a team of licensed barber stylist. Within a year her team had opened a large full service barber styling spa.

"At the grand-opening celebration, Mary announced that her barber styling spa had a highly skilled licensed staff. Mary knew that the town had complained that they could not get beauty services late at night or early in the morning and they were tired of waiting all day for a service. Mary announced that her barber styling spa was open 24 hours a day 7 days a week with no long waiting. John could only work so many hours a week and service one client at a time. Then Mary announced that she would charge 50 percent less than John did for all of his services. The town was very happy and they flocked to Mary's business. Mary got contracts with the retirement home, hospital, daycare center and funeral home to service the client's hair. Mary sent staff members to the facility to service clients.

Mary opened a barber styling school in the town and the school became accredited and started offering financial aid for students. Mary hired the barber stylist in her salons all over town upon their graduation.

John lowered his rates by 50 percent to compete with Mary and he began working 16 hours a day. He purchased two more styling chairs and trained his son and daughter to work the night shift. When his son and daughter grew up and went off to college they never returned. John had employee problems, they wanted more money and better benefits.
"Meanwhile, Mary realized that if this town wanted beauty services, the other towns must need hair care services too. She rewrote her business plan and went off to sell franchise

schools and barbers styling salons to towns throughout the world. Mary makes millions of dollars each year. Whether she works or not thousands of people attend school, while others receive beauty services.

Mary lived happily ever after. John worked behind the chair the rest of his life and never achieved financial independence.

That story about John and Mary has guided me for years. It has helped me make the right decisions in life. I often ask myself:

"Am I sitting in a chair or working behind the chair?"
"Am I working hard or am I working smart?"
"Am I making money while I sleep?"

That is what this book is about. It's about what it takes to become financially independent and freeing up your time. It's for barber stylist who are tired of working behind the chair and are ready to become financially independent.

CHAPTER 2

HOW TO ACHIEVE MORE BY WORKING LESS

Money and Time is not everything, but it is right up there with oxygen. There is 24 hours per day 1,440 minutes per day and 86,400 seconds per day, how are you spending your time.

Most barber stylist are already masters at what they are doing. You don't need more time to do the same things you are doing now. You need to do different things in order to have more time in your life. If you are like most barber stylist, you are: working an average of 50 hours per week at the salon, putting your kids in daycare so you have more time to earn money, in credit card debt, trying to earn more money by performing more services and wondering what happened to your time. You have overscheduled your life and the lives of your children. You can't seem to get ahead. You can't seem to keep up. You reach the end of each day completely exhausted, stressed out, and dreading another day, another month and another year of being in the rat race.

Yet, you are part of the most productive, most efficient workforce that ever inhabited this planet. You have technology at your fingertips, convenient foods to prepare, entertainment in your living room and 24-hour access to the world via the internet.

You are doing everything at the speed of light. You have voicemail, email, instant messaging and smart phones. You don't have to wait for anything, but yet you don't have enough time in your life.

When you think of poverty, we usually think in terms of financial poverty. But unlike financially poor people who don't have Money, however they do have TIME. Most of them have a better life than you. They don't work, their bills seem to always be paid, they are always relaxing, they spend more time with their kids, they never rush to do anything and they always seem happy. Remember, everyone has the same 24 hours each day.

Play The Right Game

Let's talk about the Barber Styling Games. In the Barber Styling Games you will learn why you are out of time. It isn't because you are overscheduled, or inefficient. It isn't because your pace of life has gotten too fast. Sure, all those things make life more challenging. The real problem is that you are playing the wrong game!

What do I mean by that? You probably think your life is supposed to be played by trading your time for money at the salon, a job or in a small business. The problem is, in that game, work takes up too much of your time. It doesn't leave enough time for you to do the really good things in life.
You need to play a game you can win, a game where the rules work to your advantage. But, you can't start doing that until you understand what the wrong games are.

Years ago, a barber stylist opened a school and everyone said he was playing the wrong game or so they thought. The barber stylist had been working behind the chair for years, but one year he decided to open a school. Instead of continuing to work behind the chair, he began to train students, became accredited and started receiving financial aid.

He started working twenty one hours per week and his income quadrupled. The headlines read, "Barber Stylist winner played wrong game." But, did he? NO! As it turned out, he played exactly the right game. If they had played the wrong game, they wouldn't have won. Many Barber Stylist play the wrong game, but luckily, the one that opened the school played the right game.

Life is like that. Most barber stylist are playing the wrong game, but, every now and then, a barber stylist comes along and does it right. Most of the barber stylist that win the game are shown an example by someone who won the game before them.

It Happened To Me!

In 1998 my life changed forever. I had opened my barber styling school in Nashville, Tennessee. I had six students enrolled at my school and it was very hard to pay the bills each month. I was talking to my mom about my pressing disappointment of the school. I wanted the school to become accredited and receive financial aid, so I could help more students, make more money. But, I just did not have the right mentor and information to do it. I couldn't seem to find the right person who had achieved what I wanted to achieve. No one was willing to help and share their knowledge.

A month later one of my friends told me about a lady name Velma Demonbreun who ran the largest and most successful cosmetology school in Nashville. I made an appointment to talk with her about helping me become successful like her. As I entered her school, everyone was happy, laughing, learning and having a great time. In fact, she was doing what I wanted to do-having fun, learning and making money. Folks, that was the moment it hit me. Up until that point, I had always thought that people in the hair industry worked long hours and never had time for themselves. But on that day, at that moment, I had a massive life changing revelation.

She was no different from me. In fact we had a lot in common. She just acted different than I did. She had what she wanted because she was playing a different game. She was playing the right game. And, if I wanted what she had, all I had to do was play the right game too.

I didn't have the things I wanted-nice vehicle, traveling, nice house, shopping, and time to enjoy myself. The game I was playing didn't go there. Even if I won my game, it wouldn't give me that kind of lifestyle. No matter how well, or how hard, or how long you play the wrong game, it will never give you the results you want. You have to play the right game to get the right results.

What Are The Right Results?

Every Barber Stylist has a different dream for their lives. You may want to enjoy a nice vehicle, traveling, nice house, shopping and more free time. You may want something else. Maybe your dream is to start a nonprofit or travel on cruises. But Barber Stylist, no matter what your dream is, you need two things: time and money. You will learn how to have both. You will learn how to create wealth without spending all your time doing it.

Most Barber Stylist are clueless when it comes to having more free time and money. They know how to make money. They go to the salon and trade their time for it. This will get you money, but not time. Most Barber Stylist know how to get more time, by reducing their hours in the salon. This allows you more time, but no money. Both systems cause a lot of stress. You are either out of time or out of money and you become stressed worrying about the one you don't have. You want Time and Money. The only way to get those results is to play the right game. You have to make changes in your life. Think different, act different, play different, choose different friends, and you can have different results. Play the game that time and money rich Barber Stylist play, and you can get what they have.

The "Hooked On Hopium Drug"

The majority of Barbers and Stylists are hooked on the drug called "Hopium". They get a job, plan to work for forty years and then hope something comes along to get them out of that work. That is why they play the lottery. They know that they will never have the time to enjoy life unless they get a miracle. They hope that they win the lottery or something big happens, because they know that what they are doing will never give them the time and money. No one they work with has time and money. Their families don't have it and their friends don't have it. They are all hooked on Hopium.

If You Win The Lottery

If you win the lottery and receive $365,000 per year for the next 20 years. You will certainly have more choices than you do now. Lottery winners win two things, money and time. If you have money, and if you get the money in a way that doesn't require you to give up all your time, you can choose to use that money in your own time.

What would you do with an extra $365,000 per year or $1,000 per day? It would certainly make life easier, you could afford to hire people to do the things you don't like to do. You wouldn't have to work overtime or an extra job. Money may not buy you happiness, but it does give you power and freedom.

What if you had to earn that money the way you do now? What if you made $365,000 per year? How much extra work would you have to do on your job to make $365,000 each year?

If you need more money in order to have more time in your life, and if you have to earn that money, and if earning that money is going to take up so much time that you will have even less time at the end of each day, then you have to earn that money some other way than earning it on a job.

Where Do You Spend Your Time?

Your time is divided into three parts: sleep, work and everything else. Eight hours devoted to sleeping or at least relaxing. Eight hours devoted to working. The last eight hours devoted to everything else like family time, raising the children, cooking, cleaning, social media, television, exercising, and so forth.

How can you find more time for yourself? I know you don't want to cut some of your personal time. You already are strapped for personal time. The only other eight hour time slots available are those for work or sleep. Do you want to sleep less or work less? You need to spend more time creating streams of income that do not require your time. If you do it right, you can work less, sleep more and still have time for more traveling and more family time.

Rules To Achieving More and Working Less

1. Get a dream
2. Study other successful people and copy them
3. Create a personal business
4. Find a system that works and apply the system
5. Retire on Mentor Equity

You'll learn how to go through these steps as you progress through this book. You will be able to spend more time doing the things you enjoy. If you do these things, you will live a different life than you do now. You will have time for the things that are most important to you. You will have a lifetime of income, without a lifetime of work.

You will not be on the 40 hour a week and 40 year retirement plan. People will value your opinion and respect you. Best of all, you will be able to retire early and enjoy life. My mentor Mrs. Velma is retired, she only does the things that bring her joy, such as giving back and helping people. There is a difference in working because you want to verses working because you have too.

Mrs. Velma helped me semi retire at an early age. I work at the barber styling school Tuesday, Wednesday and Thursday. I have a business that produces income without my presence. The other four days are spent on my personal time doing things that I enjoy doing. All this happened to me because I started doing the opposite of the majority. And all that started because I met Mrs. Velma in 1998. She woke me up and opened my eyes to a whole new world.

What will it be for you? Will you meet someone that changes your thinking and life? Maybe it will be this book. Maybe it will be our two day workshop for barber stylist. Maybe it will be a friend. Maybe you will wake up and realize that you don't have what you want and you won't get it if you keep on doing what you're doing.

How To Balance Your Life

Let's look at a typical day of most barber stylist. The alarm clock goes off. You get out of bed and you did not get enough sleep last night. You spent most of the night tossing and turning thinking about your busy day, your financial situation, kid's activities, and many other brain wrecking activities flooded your brain into a sleepless night.

You drink your coffee to give you energy and wake you up. You get the kids ready and drive them to school. You stop by a fast food place for breakfast, so your kids can eat that greasy unhealthy breakfast.

Then you go to your job all day. At the end of another day the routine day, it is time to start the rat race again. Does the day involve a nice home cooked meal? Probably not! Recent studies show that almost 90% of meals are not prepared at home anymore. When was the last time your family sat down to a home cooked meal? Who would cook it? Who would be there to eat it? After dinner, it is time for homework, social media and television. Finally it's time to go to bed, but you stay up later watching late night television show.

All most everyone is experiencing Time Poverty. What happened? Most of us grew up in a house that had more time. Didn't our parents make us home cooked meals? The truth is that most people are in time trouble. The average person barely has time to breathe, and it isn't getting better. It looks like it gets worse every year.

How To Balance Time

You can't balance your life if you haven't got the means to balance it. You can't balance your family on one side of the seesaw if the weight of the debt that you have is on the other. By trading time for dollars and then using those dollars to buy stuff that depreciates-you are working backwards.
The only thing people ever get balanced is their checkbook. Each month people look at their checkbook and wonder where all the money went.

When most people think about balancing their lives, they think about reducing the amount of work they do. If you reduce your work, you reduce your pay. If you reduce your pay, you reduce your choices in life. Soon, you more time, but you are broke. So you have to work to pay your bills, and soon you are out of balance again.

Poor people have that thinking. Many people are thinking poor! We can't imagine how to increase our wealth by working less. We try to balance our lives by doing less work, making less money, and doing fewer things we enjoy. The problem is that people try to balance their lives at the wrong level, a lower lifestyle level. Instead they should balance their lives at a much higher lifestyle level.

Most people don't understand how to balance their lives at a higher lifestyle level. For example, do teachers show us how to have a fabulous lifestyle? No, they teach us how to get the skills to work for a good company. Do our friends encourage us to pursue our dreams? No, our friends are too busy trying to keep their own lives together. What type of circle of friends do we need? You need to be the most dumb and broke person in your circle of friends. You need friends that FEED you, not FEED on you. My mentor, Mrs. Velma has mastered time and money. She spends her time giving back, helping people, swimming in her pool, talking to her husband, ridding her four wheeler and most of all having fun with her grandchildren. I always aspired to be like her and I love hanging around people like her. Association brings assimilation. If you hang around people, one or two things will certainly happen- either they will <u>influence</u> you or you will <u>influence</u> them.

How can I achieve balance at a high level? You may not want to hear this, but you got to get even more out of balance in order to make some changes. You may have to work even harder for a while in order to straighten out that see-saw at a level that gives you a more balanced lifestyle.

If you ever expect to earn more than you work for, you must first work for more than you earn!

    I made a decision that would have scared most barber stylist to death. I decided to open a barber styling school. I took the proceeds from my barbershop and <u>invested</u> in the school. Was it crazy for a while? Yes, "but I realized that I had to go out of balance if I was going to have what I wanted."

    Today I work three days per week and spend time traveling every month. I do not work on Friday, Saturday, Sunday or Monday. How long was I out of balance? Three years! "It was hard work when I started the school, but it was very rewarding. Mrs. Velma taught me her school system and after three years of really going crazy, I had it all- time, money and the friends to spend a lifestyle with."

CHAPTER 3

STARTING AT THE BOTTOM?

I cut hair in prison for three cents an hour, sodas and snacks.

I had to report to a federal the boot camp in 1995 for breaking the law. A week before my surrender date to boot camp, I went down to the federal probation office and they removed my electronic monitor from my ankle. I had to surrender at the Federal Boot Camp in Lewisburg, PA at 2pm Tuesday, May 9, 1995. They told me if I was late, I would be reported as a fugitive and I would be facing 5 years in prison. I called the Boot Camp to see what I needed to bring. They told me to bring myself and a good pair of running shoes.

    I worked in the barbershop every day until I left home a few days before my surrender date. I kissed my mother goodbye and she began to cry. I told my mother I was going to make it through for her and I would be back home in six months and get a job. I took a black briefcase with my Bible and some candy bars inside of it. I flew from Nashville to Harrisburg, PA on American Airlines. I arrived at Harrisburg, PA airport that night. I slept on the airport floor that night and I woke up early that morning and I caught a cab to the bus station downtown. I rode the Greyhound bus for about 2 hours to Lewisburg, PA.

    I was deep in the country and far away from the city. The bus dropped me off in downtown Lewisburg. I caught a cab and it dropped me off at the front door of the Lewisburg Prison. I walked slowly as I carried my brief case in my left hand. I opened the front door of the prison and a man at the front desk asked me if he could help me. I told him, I was reporting to the Boot Camp. The man told me that this was the prison (The Big House) and the average sentence here is 25 years to life. He told me, I needed to walk down to the big metal building on the eastside of this building. As I walked down to the Boot Camp facility I looked back at the prison and noticed the tall brick walls with towers sitting on each corner of the prison wall, there was a man in each tower with a rifle on his shoulder.

The place looked like a huge Army base in the lonely secluded mountains. As I entered the Boot Camp facility, I was scared and nervous. An officer told me to go in the doctor's office. I had to strip down. The doctor checked every inch of my body, including the inside of my mouth and bottom cheeks. He asked me several questions about my health. The officer came back and led me to a room, so he could issue me my clothes. I put on a green cotton jogging suit. Six months of hell was about to begin for me. The officers made me stand in one place for over 8 hours. The officers were so strict; they did everything to try to break the inmates. They wanted the inmates to quit, give up, get in trouble, and disobey rules, so they could send us to prison.

A group of first time non-violent offenders were sent to the Federal Boot Camp. We came from all parts of the United States. We came from diverse backgrounds, races, religions, and environments. It was a very tough, hard, and painful six and a half months, but also a truly learning experience. I was on the Charlie Team at the Boot Camp. Charlie Team #27 started in the blazing hot summer of May 9, 1995. During those hot summer months; I awoke at 4:30am with sweat running down my face, without the comfort of air-conditioning. At 5:00am I was out and running up hills, through hard roads, weeds, and up steps for miles. Rain, sleet, snow or sunshine, I was running.

Those runs broke many of the inmates down. Grown men would cry on those long tough runs. I ate breakfast at 6:30am. There was no talking, looking around, scratching your face or anything. After breakfast, it was time for my 17 hours a day of hard, back, body breaking and mind breaking work. During the blazing hot summer days, I dug ditches, baled hay, cut grass on hills, hoed acres of land, picked weeds by hand, squashed thousands of potato bugs by hand, picked thousands of rocks by hand, washed the rocks off, then put the rocks back in place, picked acres of beans by hand, unloaded trucks and many other back breaking jobs. There was no sitting down while working on the farm.

We drank water when the officers instructed us to drink water. The building was spotless from every square inch. I scrubbed the showers, mopped, waxed and buffed the floor every day. The floors were so shiny you could see yourself like a mirror. At 2:00pm we would go on another painful five-mile run and do numerous push-ups and exercises. Dinner was at 3:30pm every day. The food was not the best, but it was ok. 10:00pm was bedtime. Once we awoke at 4:30am, we could not sit or even touch our bed until 10:00pm.

If you were caught touching your bed, you would have to pick your entire mattress and sheets up and go outside and carry it over your head all day long. Our daily appearance was a clean-shaved head and face, spit-shined boots, heavily ironed green khaki suit with our shirt tucked inside of our pants and our shirt buttoned all the way up. We walked upright and squared every corner.

We were never allowed at any time to put our hands in our pockets or lean against anything. We sat down only when we were instructed to do so. At bedtime, it was highly humid, stuffy and hot inside the metal building, because there was no air-conditioning. Bugs and mosquitoes always bit us at night, because the windows had to be left open for air circulation. We had a small open shower room with 12 showerheads. Every night over eighty sweaty, dirty, stinky, hard working men would crowd in the shower room and take showers together.

After the blazing hot summer, the cold freezing winter arrived. We ran every morning and evening in the rain, sleet or snow, with the cold freezing wind blowing in our face. My feet and hands would be so cold, I couldn't even feel them. We shoveled all the snow off the grass onto the street and then shoveled all the snow off the street back onto the grass. The officers did everything they could to work the hell out of us. They wanted it to be an experience that we would never forget. It was freezing cold inside the metal building. Most of us slept with our hats on our heads. I would ball up under the cover every night, so I could keep warm.

Every Sunday we had a rest day to relax and receive haircuts and shaves. I was the prison barber and I was paid three cents an hour. It was the only joy that I felt while serving my time at the Boot Camp. I cut every inmates hair and I even started cutting the officers hair.

Across the street from the Boot Camp was the Federal Camp aka "Club Fed". On the other side of the street was Lewisburg Penitentiary aka "The Big House". The Big House was a city within a city. Some of the most notorious and dangerous criminals were housed there. Because of the veto (to stop disapprove) of the new Federal Crack Laws (to make powder cocaine equal in jail time to crack cocaine), a dangerous riot broke out in "The Big House". The guards used tear gas and other tactics to contain the prisoners. The guards locked most of the inmates in an underground tunnel beneath the prison. The prison was torn all up inside. Myself and many other inmates from the boot camp had to go inside "The Big House" to help the officers clean up.

We went through six tight automatic steel security doors before we actually got inside. It was an unforgettable experience for us. We cleaned the cellblocks, we mopped blood off the floors, swept human teeth up and many other heart breaking things. I saw numerous inmates locked up there. They looked like they were zombies from a movie, but these were real live human zombies with lost souls. They were mainly young men with 25 years to life in prison. Most of them were there for drugs. They had no future and nothing to look forward to or nothing to live for.

I could not believe my eyes. It looked like a dungeon inside "The Big House" that was not fit for an animal. Words cannot describe the conditions that they lived in. Society will never know. It was like Modern day or New Millennium Slavery. Their jail cells were the size of a small bathroom and they had to live in that little box cell for the rest of their lives. No amount of money or anything is worth living like they lived.

There were some very intelligent and gifted young men in prison, a few of the inmates told me to tell the world about this place, so they won't make the wrong decisions. I talked to some of the biggest and most dangerous drug dealers and criminals at "The Big House". Although the inmates were behind bars, I was very scared, because I thought the inmates were going to break out. It surprised me when those hardcore criminals encouraged me to use my talent to make money when I was released.

I called my mother on my weekly 15-minute phone call. She told me that the judge sentenced my sister to 12 months in federal prison. My sister had got her belongings to get ready for prison. On her final day of freedom the Bureau of Prisons called her house and told her that the 6 months that she served in the County jail was credited to her federal jail sentence and she did not have to go to prison. They gave her 6 months house arrest and 5 years of probation.

When I got to Boot Camp, I chose to hang around positive inmates. I did not hang with the inmates who were planning to go back to the life of crime. I met so many smart, rich and intelligent men at the Federal Boot Camp. I always wanted to know how I could be successful, without doing something illegal. I remember talking to Bill Young. Bill Young was worth millions of dollars and he was a Chinese inmate at the Boot Camp. One day Bill and I were working in the hot sun out in the fields. I asked Bill how he got all of his money. Bill told me this little story.

"If you live like your friends won't live for a few years -you will soon live like your friends can't live the rest of your life". I came to the United States over 20 years ago with no money. I moved in a one-bedroom apartment with 15 other

Chinese people. I worked 2 full-time jobs from sun up to sun down for a few years. I paid about $18 a month for my part of the bills at the apartment. I rode the marta bus to work and I shopped at thrifty stores and I took a sack lunch to work. Finally after 2 years of working very hard, I had enough money to open a little Chinese restaurant.

My business started off very slow, but it soon started to get busy. I took all of my profits and reinvested it back into my business. I soon opened a second restaurant and I started buying real estate. I finally moved out of the one bedroom apartment. I bought a mansion and a few luxury cars. Bill then told me, you people move out of your parent's house when you turn 17 or 18 years old. You get an apartment that cost $500 or more a month, you buy a car and pay $400 a month, you buy crazy tattoos, you buy expensive designer clothes, you eat out every night, charge credit cards to the limit and pay the minimum balance every month, you don't read or educate yourself, you cash checks from credit companies, you charge radios-furniture-TVs-food, and you take trips that you can't afford. He said, your people are lazy and you want everything giving to you".

CHAPTER 4

A NEW BEGINNING?

I was released from the Federal Boot Camp on November 15, 1995 and many people in Nashville were very upset. I was a man who was facing 30 years to life in prison for conspiracy to distribute cocaine.

I had two choices. I could get back in the game, make some quick fast easy money and end up dead or in prison. I could use my talent of cutting hair. Which choice would I make?

When I left Lewisburg, PA **I had Goals and a Plan on how to reach my Goals.** I also had a dream, but on the other hand, I felt scared and I felt like, I could not make it in life. My self-esteem was very low and I did not believe in myself. The warden asked me about my plans, I told him that my only goal was to help people any way I could. As I rode the Greyhound bus to Nashville I thought about everything I was going to do. It was a long 28-hour bus ride home. I knew I could not go any lower in life. I was dead broke. I knew I did not want to sell drugs, because I knew I would end up in jail or prison. I could not send my mother through all the hell and pain again. My family and a few friends had written me letters and been there for me.

When I walked off of the Greyhound bus, my mother's eyes brightened and flashed a mother's deathless love for her son. Her embrace was firm and sure. My coming home was like a miracle. I made a promise that I would use the rest of my life in a good way. I said I was going to make up for all the pain and disappointment. My mother cried for joy and she told me, I had a bright future ahead of me. She knew I was home for good. I rode around town for a few hours and my mother dropped me off at the Federal Halfway House.

Family, Freedom and a Peace of Mind was the ultimate dream come true for me. So much had happened to me in my short life. I had learned so much; I had changed my life and my thinking. I had to sleep in a big open room with about 20 other men. We each had a little bed with a small locker for our belongings. I was required to leave the halfway house in the morning but was required to return at night. Any rules broken at the halfway house meant that I would be sent back to prison. They told me, I had two months to get a job.

I told them that I could work at my friend's barbershop, but they would not let residents work with friends or family. I rode the city bus to job interviews. The mangers always asked the killer question. Have you ever been convicted of a crime or felony? I had to say yes. The managers would always ask me to explain my crimes and the managers never hired me. Two months had passed and my counselor told me that I had one week left to find a job or else I was going back to prison to finish the rest of my sentence. I was in desperate need of a job and money. I was cutting hair, arching eyebrows, performing manicures and pedicures at the federal halfway house for three dollars a service, but my probation officer wanted me to get a full time job.

I went to registration at TSU in January of 1996. I only needed 42 hours to complete my degree in Business Administration. I set a goal to take 18 hours the first and second semester and 6 hours in the summer, so I could graduate in one year. The class advisor told me, I could not complete 42 hours in one year and work full-time. The class advisor told me it would be too much work on me and I would flunk out of school. I did not let the class advisor dictate my ability or deter me from my goal. I completed 18 hours the first semester, 18 hours the second semester and my final 6 hours that summer, which allowed me to graduate from college.

I had three days remaining before my time was up. I had called my mother and I told her I had not found a job and I was going back to prison in three days. She told me to keep praying. As I was going to class, I always passed the campus salon, but I never stopped to ask them if they needed a barber, because I just knew they would not hire me. As I passed the campus salon, the voice inside told me to turn around and go in the salon and fill out an application and talk to the owner. The negative inner voice told me to keep on walking, because they are not going to hire me.

I listened to the positive inner voice and I turned around and went into the salon. I asked the owner if they needed a barber. The owner asked me if I had a barber license and I said, "yes mam". I told the owner that I had just got out of federal prison. I told her that I had changed my life and I was brought up in the church, but I strayed away like the prodigal son, but now I had come back to the Lord. I told her my parents had raised me in the church, but I got caught up in the world. I told the owner that I needed the job very bad, because they were going to send me back to prison if I did not have a job in 3 days.

The tall beautiful lady had been a hairstylist for over 30 years. She told me, "I'm going to give you this job, because you look like a good young man, your hair is cut nice and neat, your pants are pulled up around your waist and you have a belt on, your teeth are clean and white, I hate to see young men with sagging pants, braided hair and gold teeth". I had already been cutting hair, arching eyebrows, performing manicures and pedicures for all of the residents at the halfway house. Most of the residents made fun of me when I clipped the men's toenails and fingernails, they made derogatory statements, but I ignored them and continued to earn money. I told the residents that I was going to open my own barber/styling school and get my own barbershop one-day. They all laughed at me and made fun of me. They told me, I could never achieve those goals. I started working at the TSU beauty salon from 8:00 am to 4:30 pm and I attended school at night.

I did not go in the beauty salon and wait on clients, I went out and got clients. My mother made me a homemade flyer. The flyer read, "Attention Ladies and Gentlemen of

TSU, The Best Barber in the World is Cutting Hair at the Campus salon from 8am to 4pm Tuesday through Saturday". My mother gave me $100 so I could get some copies of the flyer.

I went to Office Depot and I got 4,000 black and white flyers printed. I got up at 5am the next morning and rode the marta bus to school, so I could pass the flyers out. I put a flyer under every student's dorm door, while they were asleep. I would tell myself that every flyer was $10. I did not skip a single dorm room. I then walked all over campus and taped a flyer on the wall in every classroom. I was the only Master Barber on campus and many of the students did not have transportation, so it was very convenient for them to get their haircut in the campus salon. There were 2 women that worked in the campus salon with me.

I rode the marta bus to work and school every day. I rode the marta bus back to the halfway house every night. I continued to work in the salon. My business grew very fast. I was cutting about 20 clients per day for $10 a haircut. I was making about $200 a day. I took two sack lunches to work every day. I ate one sack lunch at work and another at my evening school classes. I shopped at Goodwill and Wal-Mart for clothes. Most of the students at TSU laughed and made fun of my clothes, but I knew I had to save my money for the future. My classmates wore expensive designer clothes. Some of my old classmates asked me, where I had been and what had I been doing the past couple of years. I asked them what they had been doing the past couple of years, because I have been in trouble for the past 3 years and they were still in school. When I got in trouble 3 years ago they were seniors in my class and they were still seniors when I returned to school three years later. Most of my classmates, talked about my situation. I ignored my classmates, because I knew my situation was only temporary.

I knew I had to cut off all of my negative friends. I could not hang around the same people, because I would get back in trouble, so I cut off all of my friends off. I found myself with no friends, because none of them were good for me. My old friends tried to encourage me to hang out with them, but I told them no. My friends talked about me and some cursed me out. I stayed away from those negative people. They cracked jokes about me and called me a sellout and all kinds of names. When your negative friends turn left, you turn right.

I had enrolled back in school, because I knew education was a key to success. I knew I had to educate myself to move forward in life. I knew I needed a positive piece of paper behind my name other than a negative convicted felon piece of paper. I completed my 42 hours of college in one year. In May of 1997, my sister and I both received four-year college degrees from TSU. I remember the commencement speaker, Dr. S. Allen Counter who was the director of the Harvard Foundation. Dr. Counter was a 1965 graduate of TSU. My sister and I sat proudly in our blue graduation cap and gown as Dr. Counter spoke. Our parents were even more proud as they sat in the audience at the TSU Gentry Center.

I daydreamed that I was the guest speaker talking to the graduates. Today you begin your journey. Where will you start your journey? For many of you this is a new beginning of a new life. Forget all of the trials, tribulations and failures of the past. It does not seem long ago that I sat in your place. I was fresh out of federal prison. I said, what was next for me. I like many of you had tried the shortcuts in life and disobeyed my parents and I had to learn from experience, that there were no shortcuts in life and my parents knew everything. The only shortcut in life was education and hard work.

I always wondered what I could say to you, I can't say anything that your parents have not told you. Everyone can change for the betterment. One of the hardest things to do in life is change for the betterment. We make so many excuses instead of accepting full responsibility. Don't make it harder than what it really is, follow the yellow brick road, it is already paved. Help those that are less fortunate than you. Don't take the most precious things for granted like, family, freedom, peace of mind and good health. Don't be seduced by drugs, negative music, violence and negative people. Do not think that because, you graduated from TSU, you can't do something. The only difference in TSU, Harvard, Yale, Vanderbilt and other schools is the individual, YOU.

TSU has a great history, they have produced some of the greatest people. The richest black woman in the world graduated from TSU and people around the world told her, she could not achieve her dreams, but Oprah Winfrey proved them wrong and you can to. After the graduation, I gave my mother my degree and I told her this is for you. My mother cried for joy. I felt good, because my mother was now crying for joy. I went to church the next Sunday and the new pastor of my father's church told all of the graduates to come down to the front of the church. I stood proudly in front of the church and stared at some of the negative church members in their eyes, while my parents cheered me on. I felt good to have a college degree. I had proven a lot of the church gossipers wrong.

I went back to college and received a Bachelor of Business Administration Degree. I wrote my senior project on how to start and run a successful barber school. I worked full-time and attended school full-time. I saved my money and lived below my means by shopping at Goodwill and taking sack lunches to school and work. When I graduated from college, I had the education, experience and money to start my own business. I had to save my own money to start my own business, because the bank was not going to give me a loan. I was a convicted felon, my credit was bad from not paying credit card bills and other creditors. I knew the bank would need the last two to three 3 years of tax returns and I had been locked up, so I did not have that information.

CHAPTER 5

THE BOOTH RENTAL/ COMMISSION
BARBER STYLIST

Well, if you are like most of the barber stylist I've known, you are working for someone else, probably on commission or booth-rent. But whichever you were, you were styling, fading, arching eyebrows and shaving. And you were probably the best in the shop. But you were working for somebody else. Then, one day a strange thing happened. It might have been the paycheck your boss gave you or the way the boss treated you. It might have been the feeling that the boss did not appreciate your hard work in the business. It could have been anything, it doesn't matter what, but for some strange reason you woke up and got the Entrepreneurial Bug. And from that day on your life was never the same.

You started thinking: "Why am I working for this fool? Heck, I know more about the business than they do and I bring in all the clients. If it weren't for me, they wouldn't have a business. Any fool can have a business, because I am working every day for one." Your family members, clients and friends start encouraging you to open your own business.

The thought of being your own boss, decorating the barber salon, coming up with a cool name, searching for locations, designing a business card, all became your top priority. You would live, sleep and eat thinking about your new barber or styling salon.

Once you were stricken with the Entrepreneurial Bug there was no cure. You couldn't get rid of it. You had to start your own business. The Large Mistake barber stylist make is: if you know the physical work, you know how to run a business. And the reason it's a mistake is that it is not true. It is the main reason most barber stylist fail.

The physical work of a business and the mental work are two totally different things! But the barber stylist who starts a business does not see this, nor can you tell them. The barber stylist that has been bitten by the Entrepreneurial Bug sees the business as a place to go to work and be better than the last place they worked. So the barber stylist opens up a shop believing that by understanding the physical work of the business they are so greatly qualified to run a business that does that kind of work. And the barber stylist makes a big mistake.

Since the barber stylist is so great performing the physical work of the business, they never learn the mental part of the business. The largest mistake is when the barber stylist believes that the business that was supposed to free up their time and make them more money turns them into a slave for the business. The great cutting, fading, coloring, eyebrow arching, shaving that the barber stylist knows how to do so well becomes a burden to the barber stylist, because now they have many other jobs of actually running a business that they know nothing about. Now they are wearing every hat at their business and their strategy of owning a business has turned into a tragedy.

See the Young Man Cutting Hair.
See the Young Man Start a Barber School.
See the Young Man Die an Old Broke Barber.

I met John after he had been in business a few years. He told me, "Those last few years were worse than the prison boot camp."

John's business was named John's Barber & Style College. But, in truth, John's business wasn't really all about training men and women to be future barber stylist-it was really all about hard work. John loved cutting hair. He cut hair for three cents an hour and for snacks in prison. The work

The Millionaire Barber Stylist

John use to love to do more than anything else, plus the work John had never done in his life.

John told me, "I hate doing all this paper work, teaching the students, cleaning the toilets, answering the phone, paying all the bills, making the deposits, buying supplies, arguing with students, dealing with bad clients and I have begun to hate standing up all day cutting hair. I can't stand the crazy students.

It was 8 am and John's Barber & Style College was about to open. John had been at work since 5 am and he had already cleaned the toilets, swept the floor, mopped the floor, stocked the restrooms with supplies, made copies of registration forms, filed student records and repaired a barber chair.

I told Mrs. Mary I had been at work since 5 am and by the time I open for business, take care of customers, clean up, grade papers, file records, close up, do the shopping, wash towels, go to the bank, have dinner and be ready to open for tomorrow, it will be 10 o'clock tonight and then I got to sit down and figure out how I am going to pay the rent and power bill?

"And all my family members and friends told me to open this business because I was so great at cutting hair. I opened the school because I was tired of working for other people. I thought I was going to get paid for doing what I loved to do and free up my time to do other things".

He was in tears, but I did not interrupt him. I waited patiently to hear what he would say next. He said that he thought he was going to open up this barber styling school, train students, let the government pay him for training the students, work the students on the clinic floor, collect the clinic service money, hire instructors and then retire into the sunset. He then said, his power and water got disconnected last month for non-payment and he had to borrow the money from his mom so he could pay for the reconnection. And then he just sat quietly with his face buried in both his hands.

He was deep in debt. He had spent everything he had, and more, to open this business. The floor was black and white tile. The stations were black with matching black leather barber chairs.

He had put his mind body and soul into this place, just as he had put his heart into cutting hair. His mother would take him to the barbershop as a child and he loved the process of getting his haircut: the sitting in the barber chair, pumping the hydraulic chair up, barber draping him, putting the neck strip around his neck, fastening the drape tightly around his neck, barber showing him the mirror to see how he wanted his haircut, barber cutting his hair, edging his hairline, dusting the hair off his face, showing him the mirror again so he could see the finished haircut, dusting his face/neck with powder, applying the burning alcohol around his entire head, letting the hydraulic chair down, taking the drape off, and finally giving him a snack for sitting in the chair like a grown man.

His barber had told him, over and over again, it was the best business in the world, the oldest legal trade, you make cash each day, meet great people, watch television and give advice. John thought barbering was just about cutting hair.

I watched as John was deeply depressed and in debt. Where was his barber now? Who was going to teach him what to do next?

"John," I said in a soft voice. "It's time to learn all about the barber styling business."

The barber stylist that has the Entrepreneurial Bug turns the work he loves to do into a never ending job. The work that he previously loved becomes a stressful job that is requiring all of his time and money. He is now robbing Peter to pay Paul just so the business can survive. It has become like a train that cannot stop and you feel like you are fighting a gorilla that never gets tired. You start arguing with your loved ones, because you are unable to keep your financial responsibilities. You do not want to close the business down, because you have invested all of your money and you don't want society to think you are a failure.

I told John that every barber stylist suffering from an Entrepreneurial Bug experiences exactly the same thing.

First, a dream come true; second, lots of stress; third, anxiety attack and final, a nightmare. A sense of failure, not only failure to their clients, family members, church members, community, but failure to themselves.

John looked up at me and said, "you know exactly what I am feeling and going through." But how do I get over this mountain and eat this elephant?"

"You take one step and one bite at a time, I answered. "The barber stylist isn't the only problem you've got to deal with here."

CHAPTER 6

THE ENTREPRENEUR, THE MANAGER & THE BARBER STYLIST

The Barber Stylist isn't the only problem. There are many other problems. The primary problem of barber stylist who go into business are actually three people living in one body. The Entrepreneur, The Manager and The Barber Stylist. And the problem gets worse by the fact that each of the three people living in that one body wants to be the boss, but none of them wants to have a boss.

The Entrepreneur turns the dream into a reality. The Entrepreneur is like an eagle. The Entrepreneur patterns their life after the eagle's. There are a million species of birds that have been created by God, but the eagle is the only bird that God directly identifies himself with. God makes a few profound yet subtle statements throughout the Bible where you can see how God directly identifies himself with an Eagle. God says that there are some characteristics inside of an eagle that shares also in his own personal makeup. But they that wait upon the Lord shall renew their strength they shall mount up with wings like eagles, they shall run and not faint and walk and not be weary. In 1782 the bald eagle was chosen as our national symbol. The eagle represents distinction, honor, strength, fearless, faithful, integrity, loyalty and nobility.

An eagle is equipped with over 7,000 feathers. Eagle feathers are lightweight yet extremely strong, hollow yet highly flexible. They protect the bird from the cold as well as the heat of the sun, by trapping layers of air. To maintain its body temperature an eagle simply changes the position of its feathers. While an eagle suns itself on a cold morning, it ruffles and rotates its feathers so that the air pockets are either opened to the air or drawn together to reduce the insulating effect. Feathers also provide waterproofing and protection, and are crucial for flight. The eagle does not let the environment control what and where he does.

I have found out that most people or birds have eyes, but Entrepreneurs or eagles have vision. If you don't own anything else you should at least own a vision. Vision is the ability to see beyond your present surroundings and circumstances. Entrepreneurs use their eyes like an eagle to visualize their own business. Eagles have two foveae, or centers of focus, that allow the birds to see both forward and to the side at the same time. Eagles are the only specie that can look directly into the sun. Eagles are capable of seeing fish in the water from several hundred feet above, while soaring, gliding, or in flapping flight. This is quite an extraordinary feat, since most fish are counter-shaded, meaning they are darker on top and thus harder to see from above.

Fishermen can confirm how difficult it is to see a fish just beneath the surface of the water from only a short distance away. Eagles have eyelids that close during sleep. For blinking, they also have an inner eyelid called a nictitating membrane. Every three or four seconds, the nictitating membrane slides across the eye from front to back, wiping dirt and dust from the cornea. Because the membrane is translucent, the eagle can see even while it is over the eye. Every now and then, Entrepreneurs wipe the negative out of their eyes to see the positive.

Eagles, like all birds, have color vision. An eagle's eye is almost as large as a human's, but its sharpness is at least four times that of a person with perfect vision. The eagle can identify a rabbit moving almost a mile away. That means that an eagle flying at an altitude of 1,000 feet over open country could spot prey over an area of almost 3 square miles from a fixed position. Entrepreneurs have to be at least four times better than the average person to move beyond their comfort zone.

In studying and researching the eagle, I have discovered also that eagles never flock. Pigeons flock, ducks flock, geese flock but not eagles. The reason why eagles do not flock in other words, they don't fly in crowds or groups, because the altitude at which eagles fly is too high, most birds can't even get that high. Bald eagles can fly to an altitude of 10,000 feet. During level flight, a bald eagle can achieve speeds of about 30 to 35 mph.

To help them soar, eagles use thermals, which are rising currents of warm air and updrafts generated by terrain, such as valley edges or mountain slopes. Soaring is accomplished with very little wing-flapping, enabling them to conserve energy. Long-distance migration flights are accomplished by climbing high in a thermal, then gliding downward to catch the next thermal, where the process is repeated.

Eagles are comfortable being by themselves. When you realize you are an eagle, you will understand you don't need to be a part of no group or clique; I can stand all by myself. Obeying God will cause you to be alone. You can be alone and not be lonely. Being alone is a good thing, because when you are alone God is able to speak to you.

Another thing about eagles are they continue to fly towards their goal while they are fighting or being talked about by other birds. When conflict arises for an eagle, he does not come down on the ground to fight its prey, but rather he fights while he is in the air. Eagles only eat living flesh fresh. Eagles don't eat dead animals, you will never find an eagle on the side of the road eating out of a carcass like a vulture, an eagle will fly over that and look for something fresh. Eagles welcome storms, conflict and controversy. An eagle is the only bird that gets excited when a storm rises.

Wind storms, problem storms, people storms, financial storms and sand storms, none of that stops an eagle from flying. Eagles don't fly away from storms, but when a storm arises the eagle sets its eye on the storm and flies into the storm. Eagles don't flee from their enemies, they track them down. Eagles welcome storms, because an eagle sees a storm as an opportunity to rise to an altitude that it could have never gone if a storm had not shown up. That is why when a storm shows up the eagle sets its eye on the storm, it doesn't fly away, but it flies into the storm, because an eagle knows that it will rise above the storm.

Once paired, bald eagles remain together until one dies. Eagles are loyal with other birds; they are dedicated to their mate for life. The eagle will not accept another mate until their mate dies.

The Entrepreneur lives in the future and concentrates on their dream. The Entrepreneur is usually the only person that believes in the dream. The Entrepreneur turns their previous problems into an opportunity. The Entrepreneur often creates a great deal of chaos around him, because no one else can see the vision. The Entrepreneur view most people as average people. Entrepreneur's define average as best of the worst, top of the bottom and bottom of the top.

The Manager is like the Roadrunner in the cartoon "The Coyote and the Roadrunner." The Manager uses the six p's to success. Proper planning prevents a painfully poor performance. The Manager is the one who goes to the supply store and buys all the supplies, takes them back to the shop and arranges them in a perfect order on the shelf. The Manager makes sure all of his bases are covered. The Entrepreneur lives in the future, The Manager lives in the past. The Entrepreneur demands control, The Manager demands order.

Do you know why Wile E. Coyote never catches the Roadrunner? The Roadrunner always stays on course; he never gets off of the road, no matter what obstacles are in front of him. The Manager (Roadrunner) sees problems ahead. The Coyote sees only opportunities of catching the Roadrunner. There is one rule that pertains to that cartoon. No matter what trap Wile E. Coyote sets, the Roadrunner can never get off the track (road). Most people in business let people, problems and pain get them off track. The business will suffer when you get off track. If the Roadrunner ever got off track, he would fall off of the cliff and die at the bottom of the canyon. Why does Wile E. Coyote want to catch the Roadrunner? He wants to eat the Roadrunner. Each part of the Roadrunner's body has a very delicate taste that the Coyote can't get anywhere else in the world. Each part of the Roadrunner has an exotic taste like filet mignon, chicken, crab legs, hot fudge cake, vanilla ice cream, and ect.

The Coyote always orders his supplies from the ACME Company. I remember the Coyote ordering a rocket sled. The Coyote took the rocket sled out of the box and assembled the rocket sled together. He waited patiently for the Roadrunner to come around the curve. As the Roadrunner zoomed past the Coyote, Wile E. Coyote was in hot pursuit of the Roadrunner. As the Roadrunner ran around the narrow curve the Coyote could not successfully control the rocket sled around the curve. The Coyote ran smack into the mountain. All you heard was a whistling sound as the Coyote fell in the deep canyon.

The Coyote tried to sue the ACME Company, because he said the steering wheel and breaks were faulty on the rocket sled. The Coyote reminds me of my old self and many people in society. Every time we fell in business, we always tried to blame it on someone or something else. We also made excuses on why the business failed. The Coyote and entrepreneurs must accept full responsibility for the business. One thing I can say about the Coyote; he never tries the same thing twice after he has failed. I will give him credit for getting back up and ordering a new gadget from the ACME Company. I will also give the Coyote credit for setting his goals high and never giving up.

The Coyote could just settle for any type of food in life, he has money, he could just order a Domino's pizza or some other type of food and have it shipped over to him, but he will not settle for less. If you just stay on course in life, you will reach your goal, just like the Roadrunner. Has the Coyote ever caught the Roadrunner? Yes, he caught the roadrunner onetime. How did he catch the Roadrunner? The Coyote shrank himself down to the size of an insect and he caught the

Roadrunner on his thigh. The Coyote turned around to the audience watching TV and he said; now that I have caught the Roadrunner what am I going to do with him. When the Coyote reached his goal of catching the Roadrunner, he was not prepared to handle what he had just accomplished. If you really got what you wanted in life, could you handle it?

The manager is the one who stays on the Entrepreneur to clean up the mess. It is usually disagreements between The Entrepreneur and The Manager.

The Barber Stylist is the person that thinks no one else can do it like them. They are the doer. "If you want it done right, do it yourself" is The Barber Stylist mindset. Barber Stylist love to do everything themselves and not share their secrets. The Entrepreneur lives in the future, The Manager lives in the past and The Barber Stylist lives in the present. As long as The Barber Stylist is working in the shop they are happy. The Barber Stylist knows that if it weren't for him, the shop would be in more trouble than it already is. The Barber Stylist is the backbone of the business. If The Barber Stylist does not do the work, it will not get done.

The Barber Stylist only believes in his work, if it is not work he does, he does not want to have any involvement. It would be great if we all had an Entrepreneur, Manager and Barber Stylist to run our shop. The Entrepreneur would dream and venture into new areas of interest; The Manager could run the daily operations of the business and the Barber Stylist would be doing all the physical labor. Unfortunately, most Barber Stylist venture into business as The Entrepreneur, The Manager and The Barber Stylist all inside one body.

The average shop owner is 10 percent Entrepreneur, 20 percent Manager and 70 Barber Stylist (working behind the chair). The Barber Stylist dream becomes a reality. Out of the three bosses inside the one person, The Barber Stylist is actually in charge of the business, which is why it is headed for a disaster. There are three different personalities inside each Barber Stylist that each want something different, which creates total confusion. Can you imagine the confusion it causes in our lives? And it's not the personalities inside each one of us that confuse us but all the other people we come in contact with: our family members, friends, customers, parents, children, spouses and our employees.

A Barbers Stylist running a shop without The Entrepreneur to lead him and the Manager to supervise him, The Barber Stylist will work himself to death. He will work behind the chair from sun up to sun down each day. Only to discover that many years had gone by and he had not made any progress. "I am a Barber Stylist and not an Entrepreneur. What am I suppose to do if I don't have what it takes to be an Entrepreneur. "John there is an Entrepreneur in all of us, we just need someone to bring it out and I am going to help you bring out the Entrepreneur in you. An Entrepreneur dreams of the business, ask all the questions about why they should open a Barber Styling Salon. If you are a Barber Stylist, it is very easy for you to decide to open up a Barber Styling Salon. That's the problem. If you are a Barber Stylist and you are going to do the entrepreneurial work, you will need to change your mindset by putting the working behind the chair experience behind you and start thinking on a new level.

"You will begin to tell yourself, it's time for a change in my life, it's time for me to start making money while I sleep, it's time for me to make money without working behind the chair. And the only way it is going to happen is for me to create new business. A business that does not require me to be there every day, a business that will not drain all my energy, take up all my time, stress me out and make me a slave behind the chair. "I asked Mary, the most important question that every Entrepreneur wants to know. What can I do to create the life I desire and how can I change my experience of this business?"

"Mary said, now you are asking the right questions and let's look at where you are in business today."

CHAPTER 7

THE BARBER STYLIST FIRST PHASE

Most Barber Stylist expect their business to grow and make money. Unfortunately, most Barber Stylist businesses do not grow and make money. Instead most Barber Stylist operate according to what they want as opposed to what the business needs.

And The Barber Stylist does not want growth or change but exactly the opposite. He wants a place to go to work, free to do what he wants, when he wants, free from the constraints of working for another Barber Stylist.

Unfortunately, what The Barber Stylist wants dooms his business before it even begins.

To understand why, let's take a look at the three phases of a business's growth: Bronze, Silver, and Gold.

Understanding each phase, and what goes on in the business owner's mind during each of them, is critical to discovering why most Barber Stylist businesses don't thrive and ensuring that yours does.

The Barber Stylist opens their own business and they are free at last. Finally, you can do your own thing in your own business. Hope runs high. You dream of all the possibilities of the business. It's like being let out of a bad relationship. Your newfound freedom is intoxicating.

In the beginning nothing is too much for your business to ask. As the Barber Stylist, you're accustomed to "paying your dues." So the hours devoted to the business during the Bronze Phase are not spent grudgingly but optimistically. There's work to be done, and that's what you're all about. After all, Your middle name is Work. "Besides," you think, "this is not work for me."

And so you work. Ten, twelve, fourteen hours a day. Seven days a week slaving in your salon behind the chair. Even when you're at home, you're at work. All your thoughts, all your feelings, revolve around your new business. You can't get it out of your mind. You're consumed by it; totally invested in doing whatever is necessary to keep it alive.

But now you're doing not only doing the Barber Styling work, but you are also doing the work of a Business Owner. You have been trained to do the work of a Barber Stylist, but not the work of a Business Owner. You're not only making it but you're also buying it, selling it, and shipping it. During the Bronze Phase, you're a Master Juggler, keeping all the balls in the air.

It's easy to spot a Barber Stylist in the Bronze Phase - the Barber Stylist and the business are one and the same thing.

If you removed the owner from a Bronze business, there would be no business left. It would disappear!

In the Bronze Phase, you are the business.

It's even named after you-"JAME'S BARBERSHOP," "DEE'S SALON" and "David's Cuts & Fades," so the customer won't forget you're The Boss.

And soon- if you're lucky- all the sweat, worry, and work began to pay off. You're the best Barber Stylist. You work hard. The customers don't forget. They're coming back. They're sending family members and friends. Their friends have friends. And they're all talking about James, Dee and David. They're all talking about you.

If you can believe what your customers are saying, there's never been anyone like James, Dee and David. They work hard for their money. And they do good work. James is the best barber I ever went to. Dee is the best stylist I ever experienced. David is the smartest and fastest barber in the world. Your customers are crazy about you. They keep coming, in droves.

And you love it!

But then it changes. Subtly at first, but gradually it becomes obvious. You're falling behind. There's more work than you can possibly handle. The customers are relentless. They want you; they need you. You've spoiled them for anyone else. You're working like a slave.

And then the inevitable happens. You, the Master Juggler-Greatest Barber and Greatest Stylist, begin to drop some of the balls!

It can't be helped. No matter how hard you try, you simply can't catch them all. Your enthusiasm for working with the customers starts to irritate you. Customers, once early, are now spending many hours in the shop. The Barber Stylist begins to show the wear and tear. Nothing seems to work the way it did at first.

James's haircuts don't look the way they used to. "I said a fade not an even all over." "My name's not James; that's my brother- and I never had a high top fade!"

Dee messes up Amy's hair color: Amy wanted her hair blonde and Dee turned it orange. Amy walks out of the salon looking like the Joker on Batman.

David was once the fastest barber in the world, but his fades now have lines in the head and his razor lines are not as sharp anymore.

What do you do? You stretch. You work harder. You put in more time, more energy.

If you put in twelve hours before, you now put in fourteen.

If you put in fourteen hours before, you now put in sixteen.

If you put in sixteen hours before, you now put in twenty. But the balls keep dropping!

All of a sudden, James, Dee and David wish their names weren't on the sign.

All of a sudden, they want to hide.

All of a sudden, you find yourself at the end of an unbelievably hectic week, late on a Saturday night, still working behind the chair with 10 more people waiting to be serviced, trying to make some sense out of the mess, thinking about all of the work you didn't get done this week, and all of the work waiting for you next week. And you suddenly realize, it simply isn't going to get done. There's simply no way in the world you can do all that work yourself!

In a flash, you realize that your business has become The Boss you thought you left behind. There's no getting rid of the Boss!

The Bronze Phase ends when the owner realizes that the business cannot continue to run the way it has been. In order for it to survive and you to survive, it will have to change.

When that happens-when the reality sinks in- most business failures occur.

When that happens, most of The Barber Stylist close their shop and go back to renting a booth at another shop.

The rest go on to The Silver Phase.

John was beginning to look defeated again. I had seen that look before on the faces of countless Barber Stylist. When a Barber Stylist-turned-business-owner is suddenly confronted with the reality of their situation, a sense of hopelessness can set in. The challenge can seem overwhelming. But, I sensed that John would struggle with the idea-and himself-until he got it.

"I guess I still don't get it," he said. "What's wrong with being a Barber Stylist? I used to love the work I do. And if I didn't have all these other things, I would still love it!"

"Of course you would," I answered. "And that's exactly the point!

There's nothing wrong with being a Barber Stylist. There's only something wrong with being a Barber Stylist who also owns a business! Because as a Barber Stylist -turned -business-owner, your focus is upside down. You see the world from the bottom up rather than from the top down. You have a tactical view rather than a strategic view. You see the work that has to get done, and because of the way you're built, you immediately jump in and do it! You believe that a business is nothing more than a sum total of the various types of work done in it, when in fact it is much more than that.

"If you want to work in a shop, get a job in somebody else's shop! But don't go to work in your own. Because while you're working, while you're answering the telephone, while you're cutting/styling hair, while you're cleaning the windows, floors and toilets - there's something much more important that isn't getting done. And it's the work you're not doing, the corporate work, the entrepreneurial work, that will lead your business forward, that will give you the life of being financially independent and making money while you sleep.

"No," I said, truly enjoying this, "there's nothing wrong with Barber Stylist work; it is, it can be, pure happiness.

"It's only a problem when The Barber Stylist consumes all the other personalities. When The Barber Stylist fills your day with work. When The Barber Stylist avoids the challenge of learning how to grow a business.

"To be a great Barber Stylist is simply insufficient to the task of building a great small business. Being consumed by the tactical work of the business, as every Barber Stylist suffering from an Entrepreneurial Seizure is, leads to only one thing: a complicated, frustrating, and, eventually, demeaning job!

"I know you know what that feels like, John. Can you see that as long as you view your business from The Barber Stylist perspective, you are doomed to continue having this experience?" I asked him as gently as I could.

I saw that John was still struggling with the idea of doing what he does differently. I waited for the question I knew was brewing, and it wasn't long before it came.

"But I can't even imagine what my business would be like without me doing the work," he said. "It has always depended on me. If it weren't for me, my customers and students would go someplace else. I'm not sure I understand what's really wrong with that."

"Well, think about it," I said. "In a business that depends on you, on your style, on your personality, on your presence, on your talent and willingness to do the work, if you're not there, your customers would go to another palce. Wouldn't you?

"Because in a business like what your customers are buying is not your business's ability to give them what they want but your ability to give them what they want. And that's what's wrong with it!

"What if you don't want to be there? What if you'd like to be someplace else? On a vacation? Or at home? Reading a book? Or on a field trip with your kids? Isn't there any place you would rather be at times than in your business, filling the needs of your customers who need you so badly because you're the only one who can do their hair?

"What if you're sick, or feel like being sick? Or what if you just feel lazy?

"Don't you see? If your business depends on you, you don't own a business-you have a job. And it's the worst job in the world because you're working for a crazy person!

"And, besides, that's not the purpose of going into business.

"The purpose of going into a business is to get free of a job so you can create jobs for other people and make money while you sleep.

"The purpose of going into business is to expand beyond working behind the chair. So you can have other Barber Stylist working for you to satisfy your customers. So you can live a wonderful stress free life.

Barber Stylist usually ignore the financial accountabilities, the marketing accountabilities, the sales and administrative accountabilities. You can't ignore your future employees' need for leadership, for purpose, for responsible management, for effective communication, for something more than just a job in which their sole purpose is to support you doing your job. Let alone what your business needs from you if it's to thrive: that you understand the way a business works, that you understand the dynamics of a business-cash flow, growth, customer sensitivity, competitive sensitivity, and so forth.

"The point is," I said to him, watching his face sink and then begin to lift with an unexpressed question, "if all you want from a business of your own is the opportunity to do what you did before you started your business, get paid more for it, and have more freedom to come and go, your greed-I know that sounds harsh, but that's what it is- your self-indulgence will eventually consume both you and your business."

I paused and then continued because I could see that John was not yet totally convinced.

"You just can't get there from here! You just can't play the role of The Barber Stylist and ignore the roles of The Entrepreneur and The Manager simply because you're unprepared to play them.

"Because, the moment you chose to start a small business, John, you unwittingly chose to be a driver of the business instead of a passenger of the business. A driver can't do the same things as a passenger, because the car will soon wreck.

"And to drive this car, called building a small business that actually works, your Entrepreneur needs to be nourished, and given the room he needs to expand, and your Manager needs to be supported as well so he can develop his skill at creating order and growing the business.

"Anything less than that will eventually push you to be stressed out and, finally, out of business. Because a small business simply demands that we do it or the business will close.

"So whether we like it or not, we have to learn how. The exciting thing is, that once you begin to, once your Barber Stylist begins to let go, once you make room for the rest of you to flourish, driving the car becomes more rewarding than you can possibly imagine at this point in your business's life."

"Tell me more about that," John said. "I really want to know."

I will," I answered. "Although I sense that you already understand quite a bit more than you think. But first, let's go on to the Silver Phase, the second phase in a small business's growth."

CHAPTER 8

SILVER PHASE: GETTING SOME HELP

Silver Phase begins at the point in the life of your business when you decide to get some help.

There's no telling how soon this will happen. But it always happens, started by a crisis in the Bronze stage.

Every business that lasts must grow into the Silver phase. Every small business owner who survives seeks help.

What kind of help do you, the overloaded Barber Stylist, go out to get?

The answer is as easy as it is inevitable: Business Help.

Someone with experience.

Someone with experience in your kind of business.

Someone who knows how to do the business work that isn't getting done-usually the work you don't like to do. The clothing store- oriented owner goes out to find a marketing person.

The marketing person looks for a clothing store owner.

And so it is that you bring in your first employee-Mickey, a fifty--year-old bookkeeper/stylist who's been doing the books and styling hair since he was twenty years old.

Mickey knows the books and hair.

But most important, Mickey has twenty years of experience doing the books and styling hair in a company just like yours.

There is nothing Mickey doesn't know about your kind of business.

And now he's yours.

The world suddenly looks brighter again.

A major ball is about to be caught- and by somebody else for a change!

It's Monday morning and the Barber Styling Business is closed. Mickey arrives. You've spent all weekend getting ready for this meeting. You cleared out a generous space for him. You arranged the books and stack of unopened letters on his desk.

There's a critical moment in every business when the owner hires his very first employee to do the work he doesn't know how to do himself, or doesn't want to do.

In your business, Mickey is that person. And this Monday morning is that crucial time.

Think about it.

You've taken a big step. The books are on Mickey's desk now rather than yours.

And what's more, Mickey is about to become the only other person in the whole world who knows the real story about you and your business.

Mickey is going to take one look at the books and know the truth.

Mickey, your very first and most important employee, is about to find out a secret you've been hiding from everyone else in your life: that you don't know what you're doing!

The question is, what's he going to do about it?

Will he laugh?

Will he cry?

Will he leave?

Or will he go to work?

And if Mickey won't do the books, who will?

But suddenly you hear the quiet, systematic, clattering of the calculator's keys from Mickey's desk.

He's working!

Mickey's going to stay! You can't believe your luck.

You're not going to have to do the books anymore.

And in a single stroke, you suddenly understand what it means to be in business in a way you never understood before.

"I don't have to do that anymore!"

At last you're free. The Manager in you wakes up and The Barber Stylist temporarily goes to sleep. Your worries are over. Someone else is going to do that now.

But at the same time-unaccustomed as you are to being the Manager- your newfound freedom takes on an all too common form.

It's called Management and Delegation.

In short, like every small business owner has done before you, you hand the books over to Mickey ... and run.

And for a while you are free. After all, you still have all the other work to do.

But now that you have Mickey, things are beginning to change. But when Mickey's not totally immersed in the books, you can get him to answer the phone.

And when he's not answering the phone, you can get him to do a little shipping and receiving.

And when he's not handling a few of your customers, well, who knows what you could think of next?

Life becomes easier. Life becomes a dream.

You begin to take a little longer lunch: thirty minutes instead of fifteen.

You leave a little earlier at the end of the day: eight o'clock instead of nine.

Mickey comes to you occasionally to tell you what he needs, and you, busy as usual, simply tell him to handle it. It doesn't matter, as long as he doesn't bother you with the details. You've got hair to style, cut and students to teach.

Mickey needs more people. The business is beginning to grow. Busy as usual, you tell him to hire them. He does. Mickey's a wonder. It's great to have a guy like Mickey. You don't have to think about what he's doing; you don't have to worry about how he's getting along. He never complains. He just works. And he's doing all the work you hate to do. It's the best of all possible worlds. You get to be The Boss, doing the work you love to do, and Mickey takes care of everything else. Ah, the life of an Entrepreneur!

And then it unexpectedly happens.

A customer calls to complain about the bad treatment she received from one of your people. "Who was it?" You ask, privately steaming. She doesn't know, but if you're going to hire people like that she'll take her business elsewhere.

You promise to look into it.

Your banker calls to tell you that you're overdrawn. "How did that happen?" you ask him, your heart dropping to your knees. He doesn't know, but if you don't watch it more closely he'll have to "take steps."

You promise to look into it.

Your oldest hair supplier calls to tell you that the order you placed the week before was placed wrong, so the shipment will be two weeks late. What's more, you're going to have to eat the overage. "How did that happen?" you ask him, reaching for a Goody Powder. He doesn't know, but if you can't manage your ordering better than that, he'll have to look at other options.

You promise to look into it.

Out on the clinic floor, you walk up to a young stylist Mickey hired. He's curling a client's hair. You look at the client's hair and explode. "Who taught you to curl hair like this?" you ask the surprised kid. "Didn't anyone show you how to do this right? Here, give it to me. I'll do it myself."

And you do.

That very afternoon, you happen to be walking by the shampoo area. You almost drop in your tracks. "Who taught you to do it that way?" "Didn't anybody show you how to do it right? Here, I'll do it myself."

And you do.

The very next morning, you're talking to the new barber stylist, also hired by Mickey.

"What's happening to customer A?" you ask her. Her answer sends you into anger. "When I took care of him we never had problems like that!" "Here give it to me. I'll take care of it myself."

And you do.

And the young stylist's look at each other and ask: "Who was that?!" Mickey just shrugs and says: "Oh, that was just The Boss."

But, hear this: what Mickey knows is something you're about to learn.

That it's only the beginning of a process that occurs in every Silver Phase business once the owner's Management by Delegation begins to take its toll. It's only the beginning of a process of deterioration in which the number of balls in the air not only exceeds your ability as well.

What Mickey knows, and what you're about to learn, is that it's only the beginning of a process in which the balls begin to fall faster and with greater frequency than they ever did when you were doing everything yourself.

And as the juggling of the landing balls becomes too much, you begin to realize that you never should have trusted Mickey. You never should have trusted anyone. You should have known better.

As the balls continue to fall at an overwhelming rate, you begin to realize that no one cares about your business the way you do.

That no one is willing to work as hard as you work. That no one has your judgment, or your ability, or your desire, or your interest.

That if it's going to get done right, you're the one who's going to have to do it.

So you run back into your business to become the Master Juggler again. It's the same old story. Walk into any Silver Phase business anywhere in the world and you'll find the owner of the business busy-doing everything that has to get done in his business-despite the fact that he know has people who are supposed to be doing it for him. People he's paying to do it!

And what's worse is that the more he does, the less they do. And the less they do, the more he knows that if it's going to get done, he's going to have to do it himself. So he interferes with what they have to do even more.

But Mickey knew this when he started. He could have told you-his new Boss-that ultimately The Boss always interferes.

Mickey could have told you that the work will never be done to The Boss's satisfaction.

And the reason is that The Boss always changes his mind about what needs to be done, and how.

What Mickey doesn't know, however, is why-why you're such a madman.

That it's not your people who are driving you crazy.

That it's not the complaining customer who's driving you mad.

That it's not the banker, or the vendor, or the bad hair styles incorrectly curled that's driving you up the wall.

That it's not that "nobody cares," or that "nothing gets done on time" that's driving you insane.

No, it's not the world that's the problem. It's that you simply don't know how to do it any other way.

You're hopelessly, helplessly at a loss. For you to behave differently you would need to awaken the personalities who have been asleep within you for a long time-The Entrepreneur and The Manager-and then help them to develop the skills only they can add to your business.

But The Barber Stylist in you won't stop long enough for that to happen.

The Barber Stylist in you has got to go to work! The Barber Stylist in you has got to catch the balls! The Barber Stylist in you has got to keep busy. The Barber Stylist in you has just reached the limits of his Comfort Zone.

I looked over at John and could tell I had hit a nerve. John had discovered something in the course of our conversation-something about his Comfort Zone that was very meaningful for him.

And, intuitively, I knew we had just taken a snapshot of it.

CHAPTER 9

BEYOND THE COMFORT ZONE

Every Silver Phase business reaches a point where it pushes beyond its owner's Comfort Zone-the boundary within which he feels secure in his ability to control his environment, and outside of which he begins to lose that control.

The Barber Stylist's boundary is determined by how much he can do himself.

The Manager's is defined by how many Barber Stylist he can supervise effectively or how many subordinate managers he can organize into a productive effort.

The Entrepreneur's boundary is a function of how many managers he can engage in pursuit of his vision.

As a business grows, it invariable exceeds its owner's ability to control it-to touch, feel, and see the work that needs to be done, and to inspect its progress personally as every Barber Stylist needs to do.

Out of desperation, he does what he knows how to do rather than what he doesn't, thereby relieving his role as a manager and passing his accountability down to someone else-a "Mickey."

At that point, his desperation turns into hope. He hopes that Mickey will handle it so he won't have to worry about it anymore.

But Mickey has needs of his own. Mickey's also a Barber Stylist. He needs more direction than the Barber Stylist can give him. He needs to know why he's doing what he's doing. He needs to know the result he's accountable for and the standards against which his work is being evaluated. He also needs to know where the business is going and where his accountabilities fit into its overall strategy.

To produce effectively, Mickey needs something The Barber Stylist -turned-business-owner isn't capable of giving him -a manager! And the lack of one causes the business to go into a downward spiral.

And as the business grows beyond the owner's Comfort Zone-as the downward spiral accelerates-there are only three courses of action to be taken, only three ways the business can turn. It can return to Bronze. It can go for broke. Or it can hang on for dear life.

Let's take a look at each.

GETTING SMALL AGAIN

One of the most consistent and predictable reactions of The Barber Stylist -turned-business-owner to Silver Phase chaos is the decision to "get small" again. If you can't control the chaos, get rid of it.

Go back to the way it used to be when you did everything yourself, when you didn't have people to worry about, or too many customers, or to many bills or too much inventory.

In short, go back to the time when business was simple, back to the Bronze Phase.

And thousands upon thousands of Barber Stylist do just that. They get rid of people, get rid of their inventory, wrap up their payables in a large bag, rent a booth at a salon and go back to doing it all by themselves again.

They go back to being the booth renter, sole proprietor, stylist and hair shampooer-doing everything that needs to be done, all alone, but comfortable with the feeling of regained control.

"What can go wrong?" they think to themselves, forgetting at once that they've been there before. Predictably, this too takes its toll.

One morning-it could be weeks or years following the day you "got small" again-the inevitable happens.

You wake up in bed, and your spouse turns to you and says: "What's wrong?" You're not looking too good."

"I'm not feeling too good," you answer.

"Do you want to talk about it?" he or she asks.

"It's simple," you say, "I don't want to go in there anymore!"

Then your spouse asks you the obvious question: "But if you don't, who will?"

And all of a sudden you are struck with reality of your condition.

You realize something you've avoided all these years.

You come face to face with the unavoidable truth:

You don't own a business-you own a job!

What's more, it's the worst job in the world!

You can't close it when you want to, because if it's closed you don't get paid. You can't leave it when you want to, because when you leave there's nobody there to do the work. You can't sell it when you want to, because who wants to buy a job?

At that point you feel the despair almost every Barber Stylist owner gets to feel.

If there was ever a dream, however small, it's gone. And with it, any desire to keep very busy.

You don't wash the windows anymore, you don't sweep the floors anymore and you don't clean toilets anymore. The customers become a problem rather than an opportunity. Because if somebody wants a service, you're going to have to do the work.

Your standards of dress begin to deteriorate. The sign on the front door fades and peels. And you don't care.

For when the dream is gone, the only thing left is work. The everyday routine of working from sun up to sun down.

Finally, you close the doors. There's nothing to keep you there anymore.

And it's understandable.

Your business, once the shinning promise of your life, and now no promise at all, has gradually become a mortuary for dead dreams.

GOING FOR BROKE

The Silver Phase business has another alternative that is certainly less painful and decidedly more dramatic than "going back to booth rental". It can just keep growing faster and faster until it self-destructs of its own momentum.

"Going-for-broke" businesses are a sign of our time. With the explosion of hair schools a whole new breed of Barber Stylist has flocked to the business arena.

Unfortunately, most of these Barber Stylist barely get through the doors before the uncontrollable momentum that got them there forces them to stumble and then fall.

All the excesses of the Silver Phase, frustrating and bewildering as they might be in a normally expanding company, are disastrous in a "going-for-broke" business.

As quickly as it grows, chaos grows even faster. The Barber Stylist and his people rarely break free long enough to gain some perspective about their condition. The demand for the hair service of which they are so proud quickly exceeds their chronically Silver Phase ability to service clients.

"Going for broke" is the high-tech equivalent of Russian Roulette, oftentimes played by people who don't even know the gun is loaded!

The most tragic possibility of all for a Silver Phase business is that it actually survives!

Barber Stylist are incredibly strong-willed, stubborn, single-minded individuals who are determined not to be beaten.

You go into your business ever morning with a vengeance, absolutely convinced that it's a jungle out there, and fully committed to doing whatever's necessary to survive.

And you do survive. Kicking and scratching, beating up your people, your customers and your friends, because you've got to keep the business going. And you know there's only one way to do it: you've got to be there-all the time.

In the Silver Phase you're consumed by the business and the possibility of losing it.

And so you put everything you have in it. And, for whatever reason, you manage to keep it going.

Day after day, fighting the same battles, in exactly the same way you did the day before. You never change.

Night after night, you go home to unwind, only to wind up even tighter in anticipation of tomorrow.

Finally, your business doesn't explode-you do!

You're like a car being driven with the emergency break on, pressing the gas harder and harder only to strain the engine.

But finally, and inevitably, there's nothing left.

There's simply nothing more you can do, except face the fact that the car will not go any faster with the emergency break.

Something has to give, and that sometimes is you. Does this sound familiar?

Well, if you haven't been in business for a while, it should.

And if you haven't been in business for long, it probably will sound familiar one day.

Because the tragedy is that the phase of Bronze and Silver dominates American Barber Stylist.

It is the condition in most of the Barber Stylist we have visited over the past 20 years, a condition of rampant confusion and wasted spirits.

It didn't need to happen. There is a better way. The nerve I had touched earlier in John had diminished enough for him to collect his thoughts.

"How did you know?" he asked me quietly. "Have you been talking to someone about me?" he said, in part wanting to believe I knew more about his story than I had let on, and in part knowing he was just like everyone else.

He knew the answer. Before I could confirm it, he said, "I got small again. And I still don't understand what happened."

He looked around the salon as though seeing someone or something I couldn't.

"My Mickey was Lisa," he sighed. "I hired her when the business was only six months old. She did everything for me, Lisa did. She was absolutely incredible. I don't know what I would have done without her. She did the books. She cleaned up in the morning and after we closed. She hired my first three employees, taught them how to do the various jobs that needed to be done. She was always there when I needed her. And, as the business grew over the next two years, Lisa took on more and more of the responsibility for the business. She worked as hard as I did. And seemed to love it here. And me. She seemed to love me too.

"And then, one day-it was a Friday, July 7th, I believe, at eight in the morning-she called me and told me she wouldn't be coming in any longer. That she had taken another job. That she couldn't afford to work for what I was paying her. Just like that! I couldn't believe my ears. I couldn't believe that she meant it. I thought it was a joke. And Lisa said she was sorry. And she hung up!

"Well, I stood there and wept. And then I felt fear, a fear I hadn't ever felt before. I felt cold inside. How could this be? I thought to myself. How could someone I thought I knew so well, someone I trusted so much, have suddenly become a stranger? What in the world did this say about me? About my lack of judgment? About the conversations I should have had with Lisa but didn't?

"But the clients needed to be serviced, the floors needed to be cleaned, and the salon prepared for opening, and so, despite the pain I was feeling, the sickness in my stomach, I went to work. And I haven't stopped since. The people she hired left soon afterward. To be honest with you, I never really had a connection with them. They were Lisa's people.

"When I think back now, I see how easy it was for me to do. How easy it was for me to become absorbed by the work rather than the people. And I guess they knew that. Because after Lisa left they all seemed to regard me with suspicion.

Like I had let her go without telling them or something. If Lisa could leave, a man like that, what did it say about them for staying? At least that's what I believed they were thinking . Who knew? I was too devastated to ask. Since then I haven't had the heart to hire anyone to replace them. The thought of it is terrifying to me. The thought of bringing strangers into my life like that again feels like a risk I don't want to take. And so I do it all myself. And I know I can't do it much longer. Besides which, what's the point?

John sighed deeply and looked across at me.

" So, there's my Comfort Zone," he said. 'What do I do about that?"

"Start all over again-but differently this time," I answered. "It's the only way out of the trap."

Most of us have had the experience of being disappointed by someone in whom we have put our trust as a direct result of our indifference or lack of understanding or lack of skill or lack of attention.

And most of us learn eventually, if for no other reason than because we realize that we can't be everywhere at once, to trust again.

But trust can only take us so far. Trust alone can set us up to repeat those same disappointing experiences. Because true trust comes from knowing, not from blind faith. And to know, one must understand.

And to understand, one must have an intimate awareness of what conditions are truly present. What people know and what they don't. What people do and what they don't. What people want and what they don't. How people do what they do and how people don't. Who people are and who they aren't.

In short, John trusted Lisa blindly. John simply wanted to believe in Lisa. It was easier that way. Because if John trusted blindly, if he simply left it all up to chance, he wouldn't be forced to do the work he didn't want to do. The work of coming to agreement about what his relationship with Lisa was about. What role each of them was there to play. What it meant for John to be an owner and Lisa to be his employee. What it meant for John to set out the rules of the game that she was expecting Lisa to play.

Because John didn't feel comfortable in this new role, this role of the owner, this role of The Entrepreneur, this role of a business person, she left everything up to chance. He delegated his accountability as an owner and took on the role of just another employee. He avoided fully participating in his with Lisa, and, in the process, created a dynamic between himself and his employee built on a weak structure. An omission that foretold Lisa's inevitable departure and John's inevitable pain.

I certainly didn't need to tell John that he had no one to blame but himself. I just needed to find the right way to show him how he could do it differently the next time.

"The next time," I said, "you'll know that your business is destined to grow, and that once it does your job is going to be significantly different. For now, that's all you need.

"The true question is not how small a business should be but how big. How big can your business naturally become, with the operative word being naturally?

"Because, whatever that size is, any limitation you place on its growth is unnatural, shaped not by the market or buy your lack of capital (even though that may play a part) but by your own personal limitations. Your lack of skill, knowledge, and experience, and, most of all, passion, for growing a healthy, functionally dynamic, extraordinary business.

"In this regard, 'getting small' is, rather than an intentional act, a reaction to the pain and fear induced by uncontrolled and uncontrollable growth, both of which could have been anticipated provided the owner had been prepared to facilitate the growth in a balanced, healthy, proactive way.

"But to do that requires new skills, new understanding, new knowledge, new emotional depth and new wisdom.

A Barber Stylist that gets small again is a business reduced to the level of its owner's personal resistance to change, to its owner's Comfort Zone, waits, works and hoping for something positive to happen.

When Barber Stylist revert back to working behind the chair from failing in their business it is a big disappointment, lost investment, lost jobs of the employees and embarrassment of the business failing. The tragedy is that all this could have been avoided had the business been started differently, had the Barber Stylist approached the business in a more entrepreneurial way. "No one could have anticipated everything that has happened to you so far in your business," I said to John, "but you could have anticipated most of it." You could have anticipated what happened to Lisa and the Barber Stylist she hired.

"You could have anticipated that people would love getting their hair serviced and that the salon would grow.

You could have anticipated that growth would bring more responsibilities, more skills required, more money needed to respond to the added demand that growth always places on a business and on people.

"In short, while you could not have known everything, you could certainly have known more than you do.

"And that's your job, John! The job of the owner and if you don't do it nobody will. Your job is to prepare yourself and your business for growth. To educate yourself so that, as the business grows, you can make the correct decisions for the business. It's all up to you to make decisions about the main objectives that need to be achieved and the right people to help run the business.

The right questions need to be answered, such as: Where do I want to be? When do I want to be there? How much money will that take? How many people, doing what work, and how? What type of equipment will be needed?

You will be wrong at times and make mistakes, but you will have plans in place for the best case and the worst case.

You will have to plan and write everything down clearly, so everyone can understand it. Most Barber Stylist don't have a plan or anything wrote down on paper.

When you write a business plan, road map, set goals and looking at all the negative and positive things about the business, it is a sign of a business moving to the Gold Phase. The Gold Phase is started differently than all the other phases. The Gold Phase is founded from a point of view of the business working and prospering without you. "And because it starts that way, it will more than likely continue that way. The difference between the Silver Phase where everything is left up to you working in the salon each day and the Gold Phase where the salon operates each day without you.

"The important thing is that your experience could have been completely different. It is a completely different way to start your business than the way you and most Barber Stylist turned business owners start theirs. And that anyone can do it."

CHAPTER 10

GOLD PHASE: ENTREPRENEUR MINDSET

The best businesses are modeled after a business that works. Most Barber Stylist goes into business without a model of a business that works, but of work itself. A Barber Stylist mindset is different from an Entrepreneur's mindset in the following ways:

The Entrepreneur's mindset asks the question: "How must the business work?" The Barber Stylist asks: "What work has to be done?"

The Entrepreneur's mindset sees the business as a system for producing outside results for the customer and resulting in profits for the business. The Barber Stylist sees the business as a place to work and produce results and income for the Barber Stylist.

The Entrepreneur's mindset starts with a vision of a well defined plan on how they want their future to be in that business and they work the business to match the plan. The Barber Stylist just opens their business and works every day in an uncertain environment hoping that the business will prosper.

The Entrepreneur's mindset sees the business as a big puzzle with many pieces that must be all put together by different people to make the puzzle complete and match up with the picture of the business. The business operates according to rules and principles. The Barber Stylist sees the business as a small puzzle with a few pieces that they can put together all by themselves. As a result the Barber Stylist will soon learn that they can't put all the pieces of the puzzle together by themselves and they hire the wrong people that do not know how to put the pieces to the puzzle in the correct order. The only model that the Barber Stylist can follow is a model of working behind the chair each day.

What does the Entrepreneur see that the Barber Stylist does not see? The Entrepreneur sees more on how things are done in the business instead of concentrating on what's done in the business. How things are done in the business are more important than what's done.

When the Entrepreneur creates the model, he surveys people and ask: "What problems are you having and how can it be solved?" Having identified it, he then goes back to the drawing board and creates a solution to the problems he finds among the people. A solution in the form of a business that solves the customer's problems. The Entrepreneur ask, "How will my business stand out from the rest?" The Entrepreneur does not start with a picture of the business to be created, it starts with a picture of the customer's problems for whom the business was created to solve them and make the customers life better. It understands that without a clear picture of that customer, the business will fail. The Entrepreneur understands that there are two ways to succeed: 1. Solving peoples problems and 2. Helping other people make money.

Barber Stylist, on the other hand, focuses on the business to satisfy themselves. To the Barber Stylist, the customer is always a problem. Because the customer never seems to want to pay for what they have to offer and the customer complains when prices are raised.

To the Entrepreneur a customer is always an opportunity. The Entrepreneur knows that the customer is always changing and he is looking for solutions to satisfy them. All the Entrepreneur has to do is find out what they want and they will stay in business.

The Barber Stylist, however, the world is a place that never seems to let him do what he wants to do; it rarely appreciates his work and it rarely gets appreciated for his hard work.

The question then becomes, how can we introduce the entrepreneur mindset to the Barber Stylist in such a way that he can understand it and use it. The answer is, we can't. The Barber Stylist is busy doing other things. If we are to be successful at this, we must give the Barber Stylist information he needs to grow beyond the limitations of the Barber Stylist Comfort Zone so as to experience a vision of business that works. We must expose the Barber Stylist to people that are where they want to be and let them know about the business models, systems and training that they offer to help them get from behind the chair and start living the life they desire.

To find such a model, system and training, let us examine a revolutionary development that has transformed Barber Stylist in an astonishing way.

I call it the Turn Key Barber Styling Revolution.

It was time for John to open his barber styling school.

CHAPTER 11

TURN KEY BARBER STYLING REVOLUTION

If asked to describe the Turn Key Barber Styling Revolution, however most Barber Stylist would simply respond with a blank stare.

The Turn Key Barber Styling Revolution is a way of doing business that has the power to dramatically transform any barber styling salon or any business no matter what its size-from a condition of chaos and financial struggle to a condition of order, excitement and financial independence.

The Turn Key Barber Styling Revolution is like a McDonald's franchise. In 1952 Ray Kroc sold a milkshake machine to two brothers that had a hamburger stand in California. He had never seen anything like it. The hamburger stand worked like a smooth clock. Hamburgers were produced in a way like no other place-quickly, efficiently, inexpensively and identically. Best of all, anyone could do it. He watched kids working with precision and mistake free, happily responding to the long lines of customers. It became apparent to ray Kroc that what the McDonald brothers had created was not just another hamburger stand but a model turn-key system for running a business. Ray Kroc started franchising their method and the rest is history.

Ray Kroc created more than just a great business. He created the model upon which an entire generation of entrepreneurs have since built their fortunes. It started as a trickle when a few entrepreneurs began to experiment with Kroc's formula for success. But it wasn't long before the trickle turned into the Barber Styling Industry.

The successful businesses in the Barber Styling Industry all use a business model. All of the corporate schools and franchise salons use a successful business model.

It is the Business Format Franchise that has revolutionized businesses. The Business Format Franchise provides the franchisee with an entire system of doing business. A systems dependent business, not a people dependent business. A systems dependent business is a business that works without you being present. Ray Kroc worked on the business instead of in the business. He constructed a business that could be replicated over and over again, each business working just like the other business.

This was the perfect time for John and I to talk about the business model for his business. If he had ever felt the weight of being a Barber Stylist turned school owner, caught up in the doing of his business without making any profit, it was right now. It was eleven o'clock at night and John had just finished a very busy day. He had just finished sweeping hair off the floors, mopping the floors, cleaning the toilets, restocking the paper towels, taking out the trash, inspecting each styling station, counting the draw down, closing the credit card machine out, washing the towels and folding them.

And yet all that had gone on in the barber styling school that day, you would not have known it, the school was extremely clean. I could not help but to notice how proud John was of his school. But John was obviously very tired.

We both sat in his office and I could see it in John's eyes, he was ready for a change. Finally, he began to talk. "You talk about McDonald's as an example to be modeled. Most Barber Stylist would not agree with the McDonald's model, they think the exact opposite. How would you respond to all those other barber Stylist? "You know, John, I can sense that something has changed in you today. I can also sense that you are truly interested in pursuing this question about McDonald's and how your barber styling school can operate the same way.

I tell Barber Stylist that Ray Kroc was a man with a purpose to be successful. He lived in a regular world, like we all do, a world which most things didn't work the way they were supposed to. At McDonald's, he saw something that did wok, exactly as it was supposed to, time after time. That was inspiration to Ray Kroc. He was a very simple man.

"As certainly as you loved the hair industry, Ray Kroc loved the hamburger industry, particularly McDonald's because it produced a great result, the same way, with the same impact each time. "Now, from the outside in, I understand why you might be critical of McDonald's. You might say the hamburgers could be thicker, or less fatty, or this or that. But what you could never say is that McDonald's doesn't keep its promise. Because it does, it delivers exactly what it says it does every single time and it makes money. "So that's why I look upon McDonald's as a model for every barber Stylist. That is what integrity is all about, it's about doing what you say you will do. It has created a model that we can emulate.

Most Barber Stylist have one shop in which they love to work, styling and cutting hair every day. Ray Kroc had thousands of places touching millions of people.

"The only difference between the two of you is one physically works for money each day while the other created a system to make him money each day.

So let me tell you how he crafted something that great.

CHAPTER 12

THE BUSINESS FORMAT

Eighty percent of all businesses fail in the first five years, seventy five percent of all Business with a format succeed. The reason for that success is the pieces of the puzzle are tested before they are put in the operational of the business. Without it the business would be in a chaotic and undisciplined situation.

"Let me show you how it works." The system runs the business. The people run the system. The system is the solution to the problems that the business may encounter. The system integrates all the elements required to make the business work.

At Ray Kroc's McDonald's, every detail of the business system was first tested and then put in a people intensive business. The french fries were left in the warming bin no more than seven minutes to prevent sogginess. Hamburgers were removed from the hot tray no more than ten minutes to retain the proper moisture. Nowhere had a business ever paid so much attention to the little things, to the system that guaranteed the customer would have the same great experience every time.

Ray Kroc's system left the franchisee with little operating discretion as possible. This was accomplished by sending him through a rigorous training program at Hamburger University before being allowed to operate a franchise.

Is there a Barber Styling University to show me how to operate my business? YES.

The International Barber & Style College is located in Nashville, Tennessee. They have a two day course that teaches the Barber Stylist how to run the system to operate their business. Once the Barber Stylist learns the system, they are given the key (manual) to their own business. Thus, the

81

name: Turn Key Operation. Velma has designed the business well, every problem has been thought through. All that's left for the Barber Stylist to do is learn how to manage the system. Barber Stylist travel from all over the United States to learn the system on operating a successful Barber Styling School.

John asked "Why are Barber Stylist traveling all over the United States to attend this two day seminar to learn this system?" They want to "Retire From Behind The Chair" and move to the next level.

What is covered in the system?
How to Start, Run, Grow A Successful School
How To Get Accredited
How To Receive Government Grants
Live Hands On Training

Things Covered in the System

- Organizational Chart
- School Opening & Closing Checklist
- Perfect Student Checklist
- Receptionist Front Desk Procedure
- Receptionist Front Desk Checklist
- Cash Register Operator Report
- Customer Sign In Sheet
- Price List Sheet (Clinic Services)
- School Sign (Services By Supervised Students)
- State Board Inspection Sheet
- Now Enrolling Sheet (For Students)
- Advertisement Business card
- Advertisement Postcard
- Chemical Release Form
- Admissions Enrollment Procedures
- Grant/Enrollment Checklist
- Catalog
- Student File Checklist
- Student Registration Form

- Reference Sheet
- Orientation Verification Sheet
- Student Kit List
- Tuition Contract
- School Loan Agreement
- Hold Harmless Agreement
- Attendance Sheet
- Theory / Practical Completion Sheets (Cosmetology)
- Full-time Syllabus (Nail Tech)
- Part-time Syllabus (Nail Tech)
- Theory / Practical Completion Sheets (Nail Tech)
- Full-time Syllabus (Natural Hair)
- Part-time Syllabus (Natural Hair)
- Theory / Practical Completion Sheets (Natural Hair)
- Full-time Syllabus (Aesthetics)
- Part-time Syllabus (Aesthetics)
- Theory / Practical Completion Sheets (Aesthetics)
- Theory/Practical Completion Sheet (Instructor)
- Theory / Practical Completion Sheets (750 hours Cosmetology /Barber)

- Full-time Syllabus (750 hours Cosmetology /Barber)
- Part-time Syllabus (750 hours Cosmetology /Barber)
- Student Progress Report
- Monthly State Board Student Hours Report
- Student Evaluation of Institution (Current Student)
- Graduate Student Survey
- Employer of Graduate Survey
- Cosmetology Program
- Nail Program
- Aesthetics Program
- Natural Hair Program
- Cosmetologist Program For License Barber Stylist
- Instructor Course Objective
- Cosmetology Practical Test
- Nail Tech Practical Test
- Natural Hair

- Instructor Practical Test
- Grading Scale
- Employee Evaluation
- Student Advising Form
- Student Complaint Form
- Student Withdrawal Form
- Internal School Complaint Procedure
- Internal School Complaint Committee
- Class Schedules
- Staff Phone Numbers
- Substitute Teachers
- Emergency Numbers
- Contact Numbers
- Voice Mail Phone System
- Emergency Plan
- Job Descriptions
- Schedule Holidays & Staff Meetings
- Record of Fire Drills
- Continuing Education for Instructors
- Policy on Reviewing Student Files
- Attendance Policy
- Refund Policy & Example
- Request Leave Of Absence
- Policy on make-up hours
- Patron service procedure
- Refund check acknowledgement
- Refund calculation sheet
- Request for transcript
- School Supply List (Maintenance)
- Student Approval List For School
- Employee Handbook

So now you have it: the system is a model you've been looking for. The system is a model that works. The balanced model that will satisfy the Bronze, Silver and Gold Phase. All successful businesses use a system. It's been there all the time! It's been there at McDonald's, Federal Express,

Subway, KFC, Taco Bell, UPS, Aveda, Paul Mitchell and many more. It's been there waiting for you to discover it, all this time.

Because, after all, that's all that any Business Format really is - It is a way of doing business that successfully differentiates every extraordinary business from every one of its competitors.

The question is: How do you build yours? How do you put this powerfully liberating idea to work for you? How do you create your Prototype? How do you, like Ray Kroc, build a business that works predictably, effortlessly, and profitably each and every year?

How do you build a Barber Styling School that works without you?

How do you get free of your business to live a fuller life?

Do you get it? Do you see why it is so important? Because until you do it, your business will control your life!

But once you begin to put this idea to work for you, you're on the way to being free!

I could see that John finally got it. John wanted to do in his business what Ray Kroc had done in his. All he needed to do was learn how!

CHAPTER 13

BARBER STYLING SCHOOL BUSINESS PLAN

Barber / Cosmetology School Business Plan

Starting Your Business

Businesses are born of dreams. Many first-time entrepreneurs have always longed to be their own boss. Some aspire to financial independence, while others are more concerned with blending their work with a certain lifestyle in a particular location. Whatever your dream, making it come true takes planning and following a simple formula. By following the suggestions outlined in the following chapters, you'll be heading in the right direction.

Assess and Reduce Risk

Researching similar businesses. Look at their locations, advertising, staff requirements, hours they're open, and equipment.	
Knowing your strengths and preferences. Does it capitalize on your strengths? Can you fill in the areas that you have little or no expertise in with staff members, partners or consultants?	
Examining your family budget. How big a financial cushion do you have, in case your financial projections show that you won't be able to draw a paycheck for the first year? What income can you reasonably expect while you are in the start-up phase?	
Knowing how change in the economy will affect your business. How has your type of business performed in various economics conditions? If the business is a seasonal one, will patrons of your business travel or spend less?	
Writing a business plan. Your business plan will help you shape your business, determine your financing needs, evaluate your competition, and figure out marketing strategies. It enables you to foresee problems and make a plan to avoid them. It is a valuable management tool in running your business.	

Notes:

How Much Money Will You Need To Start?

Rent. Under many lease agreements, you'll be expected to provide the first and last month's rent plus security deposit.

Phone and utilities. Some telephone and utility companies require deposits, while others do not.

Equipment. Equipment costs vary from one business to another. At a minimum, most businesses need office equipment, signage, and security systems. To determine your costs, list all the equipment you must have to efficiently operate your business. Next, price those items by obtaining quotes or bids form at least three vendors. Use the quotes you receive to estimate your start-up equipment costs. Ask about lease purchasing equipment to save money in the beginning stages of your business.

Inventory. Like equipment, inventory requirements vary from business to business.

Leasehold improvements. These non-removable installations, either original or the result of remodeling, include carpeting and other flooring, insulation, electrical wiring and plumbing, bathrooms, lighting, wall partitions, windows, ceiling tiles, sprinkler systems, security systems, some elements of interior design, and sometimes heating and/or air-conditioning systems. Because the cost of improvements can vary tremendously, get several estimates from reputable contractors.

Marketing budgets. Most companies determine their first year's advertising budget as a percentage of projected gross sales, typically two to five percent.

Licenses and tax deposits. Most cities and counties require business operators to obtain various licensees or permits to show compliance with local regulations. Licensing costs vary from business to business, depending on the requirements of your particular location. In addition to these fees, you'll also need start-up capital for tax deposit against future taxes to be collected.

Professional services. Before you officially open your business, get help from a knowledgeable lawyer and accountant who work with small business owners to make sure meet your legal and tax obligations. Their fees will range according to their expertise, and the location and size of their practices.

Pre-opening payroll. If your business is going to be a full-time venture, then set aside a salary for yourself in addition to a three-month reserve, just to play it safe. This rule of thumb also applies to any employees you might hire during this phase of business start-up.

Insurance. Plan on allocating the first two quarters' cost of insurance to get your business rolling.

Don't forget to add a "rainy day" or contingency fund to cover the costs of unforeseen expenses. This financial cushion will help you – and your investors – avoid panic in case you're faced with an expense you hadn't budgeted for.

Notes:

Failure Factors	
• Running out of money	
• Lack of business planning	
• Inefficient control of costs and quality of product	
• Insufficient inventory control	
• Under pricing of goods sold	
• Poor customer relations	
• Failure to promote and maintain a favorable public image	
• Bad relations with suppliers	
• Terrible management	
• Illness of key personnel	
• Reluctance to seek professional assistance	
• Failure to minimize taxation through tax planning	
• Inadequate insurance	
• Loss of key personnel	
• Lack of staff training	
• Insufficient knowledge of the industry	
• Inability to compete	
• Failure to anticipate market trends	
• Inadequate cash-flow control	
• Growth without adequate capitalization	

•	Ignoring data on the company's financial position	
•	Incomplete financial records	
•	Overextending credit	
•	Over borrowing	
•	Overdue receivables	
•	Excessive demands from creditors	

Notes:

Learn About the Competition	
• Advertising and promotion	
• Sales tactics	
• Distribution channels	
• Pricing strategy	
• Size of business and number of employees	
• Strategic partnerships with key suppliers	
• Customer service programs	
• Clip and save all ads of your competition	
• "Shop" competitors by visiting their business or by placing orders	
• Get copies of their letterhead, , brochures, and printed material	
• Visit their website	
• Visit trade shows to see what your competitors are up to	
• Send out questionnaire to prospective customers	

Notes:

Industry Structure	
• Competition between firms	
• Determine the number of competitors in the industry, their size and location	
• Threat of competition from potential entrants	
• Determine the buying power of customers	
• Determine the cost structure of an industry	
• What do customers want	
• What needs are not being met	
• What new strategies are your competitors starting to employ	

Notes:

Your Business Location
• Is the population base large enough to support your business
• Does the community have a stable economic base to support your business
• Close to a chain or department store
• Close to good schools and public services
• Well-maintained business and residential premises
• Good transportation facilities with access to other parts of town
• Location of business must be convenient for customers
• Check for restrictive zoning ordinances
• Find out about previous businesses that occupied the site

Notes:

Location Checklist

Is the facility large enough for your business	
Does it meet your layout requirements	
Does the building need any repairs	
Will you have to make any leasehold improvements	
Will you have to do any electrical, plumbing, or ventilation work	
Is facility easily accessible to your prospective clients or customers	
Can you find qualified employees	
Is facility consistent with the image you would like to project	
Will neighboring businesses patronize your business	
Are any competitors located close to the facility, if so can you compete	
Are the lease terms and rent favorable	
Is the location zoned for your type of business	
Does site have adequate parking	

Notes:

Lease Checklist	
Is there sufficient electrical power	
Is there enough parking for customers and employees	
Is there sufficient lighting, heating and air condition	
Do you know how large and what kind of sign you can put at your facility	
Will the city's building and zoning departments allow your business to operate in the facility	
Will landlord allow the alterations that you deem necessary for your business	
Must you pay for returning the building to its original condition when you move	
Is there any indication of roof leaks	
Will codes approve your business at this location	
Will the fire department approve the operation of your business at this location	
Do you have written guidelines for renewal terms	
Do you know when your lease payments begin	
Have you bargained for one to three months of free rent	
Do you know your date of possession	
Have you listed the owners responsibility for improvements	
Do you pay the taxes	
Do you pay the maintenance fee	
Have you asked your landlord for a cap of 5 percent on your rent increase	

Have you retained the right to obtain your own bids for signage	
Have a real estate attorney reviewed your contract	

Notes:

Before Signing the Lease	
Talk with previous tenant	
Have a building maintenance man to fully inspect building	
Inspect air condition/heating unit	
Inspect insulation of building	
Inspect plumbing	
Inspect electrical	
Call all utility companies for a print out of previous bills	
Check on all licenses (county, state, federal, ect.)	
Check on all permits (fire department, sign, ect.)	
Check on all zoning ordinances	
Sign a short lease with option to renew	

Notes:

After Signing the Lease	
Open Corporation	
Take corporate license to obtain business license	
Obtain employer identification number (EIN)	
Open business bank account	
Have insurance	
Have utilities turned on	
Have alarm installed	
Install outside sign	
Complete build out	
Set up equipment	

Notes:

Leasing Versus Purchasing Equipment Checklist

Cost	Lease	Purchase
What down payment is required for the lease or loan		
What is the length of the lease or loan		
What is the monthly payment of the lease or loan		
Are there balloon payments associated with the lease or loan		
What is the amount of the balloon payments		
What is the cost of an extended warranty, if purchasing one		
What is the total cost of the lease or loan (including maintenance and warranties) over its lifetime		
Cash Availability	**Lease**	**Purchase**
Is there sufficient cash flow to handle the monthly lease or loan payments (answer yes or no)		
Are maintenance costs included in the lease or loan		
What maintenance costs are associated with the item		
Tax Benefits	**Lease**	**Purchase**
Can the item be depreciated for tax purposes in a lease or loan		

Leasing Versus Purchasing Equipment Checklist		
What is the depreciable life of the item		
What is the estimated depreciable expense of the item over its depreciable life		
What is the amount of other tax benefits associated with this item		
Obsolescence	**Lease**	**Purchase**
What is the operable lifetime of the item		
What is the total cost of the item spread over this lifetime (divide cost by lifetime)		
What is the technological lifetime of the item		
Will the item need to be replaced due to technological advancement		
What is the total cost of the item spread over technological lifetime (divide cost by lifetime)		

Notes:

Barber & Style School Business Plan

An Example for a Start –up Hair School or Salon Business

Barber & Style
Excellent Hair Service!
Barber & Style, Inc.

Address
City, State, Zip Code
Phone Number
Email
website

Barber & Style, Inc.

This business plan for a hair school supports its commitment to a dynamic, cutting-edge, hair care and training college establishment by using an energetic and lively format. The aggressive scheme of expansion and watertight description of all aspects of the business contribute to the innovative and elite image being conveyed by the business. This plan is testament to the value of extensive forethought, as it outlines the business direction for the next 15 years.

VISION/MISSION

COMPANY OVERVIEW

PRODUCT STRATEGY

MARKET ANALYSIS

FINANCIALS

Barber & Style Business Plan
VISION/MISSION

The name of the corporation is Barber & Style. The theme is urban, industrial, techno and chic. The first question that rises for most is, "What does it mean?" If you asked that question, know that you probably are a baby boomer and haven't been watching MTV or ESPN, where mass symbols and visualization play an important part in marketing. We refer to it as being, "hip and cool" and that is what Barber & Style is, "a hip cool service, product and training center for barber styling for the people of Florida. Florida's population is growing every year. The educational center will be an elite school of barber & styling, servicing to a class of 100 every 12 months. This will serve 2 purposes:

1. Basic training for the industry focusing preparing students for the hair industry.
2. Service the price conscious economy in the Florida area.

Barber & Style is the only training center in the Florida area. Barber & Style the hair school offers a full line of products noted for their commitment to the environment. As a concept school for Barber & Style is allowed to carry products other salons and schools do not. The front of the school is committed to being a strong retail center, inviting shoppers to interact. The target is 35% retail sales to service dollar sales. Barber & Style is the only area hair school to be online and fully automated. International will have the most aggressive marketing campaign of any other area salon.

Barber & Style is in its infant stage, however, it carries goodwill from previous business in respect of the hair industry. Both Mary, the vice president of Barber & Style, and I have strong backgrounds in business and retail management. A school will complete the 4 major areas of business. To summarize, the areas of business will include barber styling school training men and women, a retail center, clinic floor servicing men/women/children, and an educational center. The target market will be the young professional, children, senior citizens, college students and people interested in saving money. The school will be marketed to the price conscious in the clinic and will be an elite school for basic training in barber and styling.

The challenges for the industry are the same challenges for Barber & Style. These are recruitment, retention, and productivity. Being a native of the Florida area, where I received my barber styling and instructor license in 20XX, I know the area businesses, high schools and people who work at them.

Retention is a problem for school and salons that lack structure and management. Both Mary and I have owned and operated successful businesses. Productivity is assessed through employee evaluation by way of salon management software. Client retention, retail dollar to service dollar sales, and goals are all part of the productivity picture. Veteran stylists and instructors are attracted to employers who offer flexible hours and adding to their education by becoming instructors. The Barber & Style College will supply a guaranteed hourly rate for new talent, thus keeping payroll predictable for management purposes. Productivity will be monitored through automation. It is realistic to believe that each department can operated at 80% productivity for top-end projections.

Financing is 100% from a financial institution. A total of $400,000 is needed to safely start and grow the business, keeping interest secure and the business healthy. Ten percent or $40,000 will be put into savings for security.

Barber & Style College's vision is to create a profitable, productive, educational school environment, supplying the community with a great vocational school, retail center and hair and nail center.

The mission statement is very clean in the approach: Having fun doing business by sharing the passion of barber styling technology, art, and science.

Future planning includes, expansion of more barber styling schools and salons. The schools will conduct morning, evening and weekend classes, maximizing productivity. We will also conduct advanced training for licensed barbers and stylist.

Barber & Style College, Inc. was founded in 20XX and is presently in its start-up stage. Barber & Style can be best described as currently being in the business of barber styling, education, and wellness. In recent times our key strengths have been customer service, retailing, and education, teaching the most recent technological aspects of barber styling and business salon management. The corporation brings together talent with educators in barber styling and business that each have more than 15 years experience in the industry.

To profile the issues of the president and vice president, it is the responsibility of management to increase profitability, improve productivity, motivate and inspire associates, create promotional calendars, increase student/client retention by way of maintaining the policies and procedures, conducting evaluations, and controlling the numbers. Annual board meetings will set the fiscal year with goals, review of policies, and share worth. An advisory board will enhance objectivity and provide guidelines to corporate directors.

Corporate directors will also be employees of the corporation. Tim will head the clinic floor department, William will head the education department, and Sue will head the financial aid department.

Growing professional barber stylist is the focus of the mission. Entry-level barber styling positions require strong technical skills, strong communication skills, and strong sales. In addition to these skills, barber stylist need to be trained in personal financial management and estate planning. Maslow's hierarchy theory states that after survival, when basic needs are met, one can go to higher levels. Our commitment is to have fun doing what we love and be profitable at the same time, while growing the business long term and committing to the personal development of pour people. This will help improve the image of the industry. This will attract the best barber stylist in our area. It is our vision of harmony for the community.

The mission statement also states that this is achieved by combining technology, art and science. International will use automation to retain students and clients. It takes 3 times the amount of effort to attract a new client versus the effort required to retain a happy client. Professional School software makes direct marketing a breeze. Presently, 20% of all barbers styling schools are automated. Locally, 5 schools are automated and none use the technology to market and track clients. Automation is key to growing and maintaining our target market.

Goals and Objectives

It is the goal of Barber & Style College to provide the community with an institution of barber styling that targets all socioeconomic standing and is a model for the industry nationally. This models the Barber & Style College's objective, placing an emphasis on personal as well as environmental wellness. It is this objective that ties together the school, the retail center and salons.

The Ten Commitments of Excellence

1. Commitment to well-being
We believe well-being is the cornerstone of personal and professional growth. Without personal and professional well-being our mission cannot be achieved.

2. Commitment to the team objective.
We believe in total commitment to the team. The team objective is a guide for us to follow in our service to our clients, support of each other, and team growth.

3. Commitment to goal attainment.
We believe every individual should have personal economic goals. Students and staff work within a framework of daily evaluation in order to identify and achieve their long-term objectives.

4. Commitment to our time management system.
We believe our time management system should be utilized in all clinic activities to provide maximum efficiency and effectiveness for our clients. We commit to managing our time and setting specific goals within that time.

5. Commitment to excellence in all we do.
With our philosophy we become team members, working for ourselves and each other. We have high expectations in terms of conduct, and know that each of us is a reflection of the team.

6. Commitment to incredible, outstanding, unbelievable client service.
We believe in extending such incredible service to all clients that they fell like honored guests in our establishment. We constantly anticipate, meet, and exceed our client's expectations.

7. Commitment to retailing through client experience.
We believe that each team member is also a salesperson. Retailing is vital prerequisite to client experience and ultimately leads to professional success.

8. Commitment to value-added service.
Value-added means doing and giving more than is expected. We believe each us needs to go above and beyond the call of duty. The school and salon will benefit in direct proportion to the value-added service provided by each team member.

9. Commitment to innovation.
We believe our strength lies in our passion to implement new ideas and embrace change. We realize that innovation involves risking failure. But we choose to risk failure in our pursuit of success rather than fail passively.

10. Commitment to personal property.
Commitment to respecting all equipment and belongings of others (as well as to the Barber & Style College). Stealing from others is stealing from oneself.

Through strong commitment. Strong marketing, and a solid financial plan, International will service the community and be recognized as a business leader. We feel very confident that the goals can be reached.

Legal Business Description

The legal name of the company is Barber & Style College Inc. The legal form of the business is Subchapter S Corporation. Refer to article papers submitted to the state, July 1, 20XX. The business location is in Orlando, Florida.

Management Team

Our management team consists of people that have mastered their technical skills and have a desire to share that knowledge with new talent entering the industry. Career experience expands over three decades.

Flowchart for team members is available for in-house management. Other charts will explain roles and responsibilities along with compensation of each position available at International. This includes the roles and responsibilities of James, the president, and me, the vice president.

Flowchart for team members is available for in-house management. Other charts will explain roles and responsibilities along with compensation of each position available at International. This includes the roles and responsibilities of James, the president, and me, the vice president. This does presently include the school staff and its management team.

The outside management team consists of Dale Smith, accountant and Jim Johnson, corporate lawyer. Our outside management advisors provide tremendous support for management decisions and creativity.

By January 20XX an advisory board, including two highly qualified business and industry professionals, will assist our management team is making appropriate decisions and taking the most effective action; however, they will not be responsible for management decisions.

Staffing

The Barber & Style College team recognizes that additional staff is required to properly support our growth. Presently, there are five people on staff. We are currently interviewing for new staff. As a teacher of barber styling, I have seven years of former students that hold barber styling license positions in the community. Growth opportunities improve employee retention within our industry. International recognizes the need for growth of the individual.

President and Vice President

As executive officers of The Barber & Style College, it is our responsibility to improve the image of our industry through solid business management. This is achieved through increasing profitability for the business, its officers, and staff. It means improving productivity for each department. Motivating and inspiring management, technicians, and associate staff with leadership will improve the image, as well as having fun sharing the passion for barber styling combining technology, art, and science.

To grow a healthy business is to continually assess the needs of the people who hold the same vision creates a harmonious, productive, and profitable salon environment. It is our responsibility to be committed to this process.

Responsibilities:

James, President
- Retail center. Oversee the operations of the retail area. This includes inventory, stocking, and displays.
- Oversee receptionist duties and scheduling.
- Oversee the Clinic floor operations.
- Participate with instructors. Managers should report to Chin for needs.
- Handle payroll operations.
- Participate with interviewing.
- Act as school manager until department can support a head.
- Develop color specialization.

Mary, Vice President/Financial Aid Director

- Educational director for Barber & Style College.
- Process student financial aid
- Marketing planner.
- Staff meetings.
- Oversee goals and evaluations
- Co-associate program.
- Develop Barber & Style College. Com web page and future shopping center.
- School technology and training.
- Participate with interviewing.
- Number cruncher.

Educational and Experience:

Refer to resumes and portfolios.

Compensation:
It is the responsibility of the officers to provide themselves with a comfortable wage. However, these wages will not take away from the business. The business then is paid first with a formulation of 15% from the gross. This ensures a healthy business growth. Also in this formulation is reward for long term employment with shares given and retirement plans for its staff members. A financial advisor will help with the education needed for benefit of all. Growth is a process. We are committed to this process.

Role: Theory Instructor
As the instructor you hold a strong leadership position within the company as well as within the community. By carrying out the company's vision and mission on a daily basis, you will ensure a harmonious, productive, creative, and profitable school environment. You will instill the importance of our mission of having fun doing business by sharing the passion of barber styling combining technology, art, and science with the students and co-associates who in turn will share this with their clientele.

Responsibilities:
- Be able to teach theory in the classroom and determine at what point a student should work on the client floor. This program must be educationally rewarding to the student. The educational process for the co-associate must be measurable with a competency based closure.
- Record student grades and submit to school director.
- Monitor the orientation of the student and evaluate the progress.
- Self-direction and education will be a must, keeping up with latest trends. The staff will look to you as the fashion leader.
- Active involvement in recruiting and interviewing potential staff.
- Coordinate training and development between departments.
- Attend department head meetings on a quarterly basis.
- Participate in staff meetings on a quarterly basis.
- Continually furthering your education. It will be expected that you attend one seminar annually. Education is key to profitability.

Education and Experience:
An endorsed high school diploma. Three years experience in the field of barber styling. Attendance at an advanced class of education committing to updates on a national level annually. Minimum overall service sales of 25% in chemical services. Public speaking skills as needed to communicate trends to the students.

Compensation:
This is an optioned position, whichever produces the most revenue for the director. Once this option is made, it holds in place for one year before review.

Option 1:
- Salary based at $9.25 hourly for this full-time position. This is also a stipend position paid bi-annually based on 80 hours per year with staff and co-associate training and development. The pay for the stipend is derived from average weekly pay over a 6-month period.
- Bonus program. Productivity bonus of 2% for each department hitting 100% of service goal or 1% bonus for 80% reach of goal.
- Individual retail sales commissioned at 10%.
- Paid vacation. One week paid after 2 years service. Two weeks paid after 5 years service.
- Health insurance, 50/50 pay after 90 days.

Role: Receptionist
A school receptionist is a viable position to a successful and harmonious school. You, as the receptionist, give the first impression and the last impression to everyone who passed through the front door. All clients and customers come first and it is your responsibility to create a balance of all daily duties. It is also your role to facilitate the vision of having fun doing business by sharing the passion of barber styling combining technology, art, and science and to communicate that vision to the clientele.

Educational Requirements: Endorsed high school diploma with a background in basic computer skills. Related customer service experience is also necessary.

Compensation Base: An annual salary of $XXXXX is a base for this full-time position. Performance is to be rewarded. Meeting retail sales goals by 100% results in a 2% bonus. Meeting retail sales goals by 80% results in a 1% bonus. Payment of bonuses will be given through quarterly evaluations. Paid vacations are given with years of service. One week paid after two years and two weeks paid after five years of service.

Health insurance is to be self-funded. Group rates are available.

Part-time employees are given a flat rate hourly plan at $6.00 per hour.

Responsibilities:
- Customer service. Greet all clients and customers within the first 10 seconds with a smile. Make them feel welcomed and comfortable. Offer a beverage, reading material, and take their coat. Direct them to a dressing area if appropriate.
- All new clients are given a menu and tour of the facilities. If you are unable to do so, find an associate who is available, introducing them to the client by name.
- Handle all phone calls politely and professionally using your name when answering the call.
- Booking appointments. Taking client's name, phone number, and type of service. Repeat the time, day, and date appointments to client. Resource information for available time to book appointments of each technician.
- Confirming appointments. Appointments for the following day are to be confirmed by the end of the shift.
- As a receptionist, you will be responsible for handling all financial transaction of clients. You will have a complete understanding of the POS terminal as well as the credit card terminal and their functions.
- Gift certificates will be issued, monitored, and filed by the receptionist on duty.
- Proper maintenance of change in the cash drawer is expected.
- New inventory shipments will be promptly checked into stock.
- The answering machine is to be attended to every morning and the calls returned immediately.

- It is the receptionist's duty to close out the POS terminal and credit card terminal at the end of the day or shift.
- Maintenance of the reception area, waiting area, and display units are also responsibilities.
- Inform students when their clients have arrived or canceled.
- Day runners will be given with data cards each morning.

Role: Floor Instructor

The main responsibility of the Floor instructor is to encourage, inspire, motivate, and train students on the clinic floor. This is achieved through relaying the vision and mission of International, creating a school environment that is harmonious, productive, and profitable. Having fun doing business by sharing the passion of barber styling combining technology, art, and science is the mission of International. The instructor who models this vision and provides support in the mission will be a strong leader. It will be your responsibility to be this leader.

The instructor will help guide and find solutions for the student if problems should arise. Being a leader in the company, you will ensure customer and student service to its fullest potential, thereby maintaining client and student retention and achieving retail goals.

Responsibilities:
- Active involvement in training each student.
- Orientation of new floor instructors, job description, policy, and procedures of International.
- Making sure that clients are getting the best customer service.
- Ensure all students are supplied with business cards.

- Handle customer complaints and suggestions from the clinic floor in a pleasant, efficient, and professional manner.
- Focusing on clients' needs first. This cannot be stressed enough. Listening to verbal and nonverbal cues is imperative to client retention.
- Continually furthering your education. It will be expected that you attend one seminar annually. Education is key to profitability.
- Attend department head meetings on a quarterly basis.
- Participate in presenting staff meeting on a quarterly basis.
- Evaluate clinic floor monthly. This includes reviewing client retention and productivity in service and sales.
- Keep inventory of supply room.

Floor Instructor will be responsible for receptionist duties, until the Clinic Floor is productive enough to support the investment of a receptionist. This included nightly drawer closing.

Education and Experience: An endorsed high school diploma. Three years experience in the field of barber styling. Attendance at an advanced class of education committing to updates on a national level annually.

Compensation: This is an optioned position to be chosen at time of employment. It is to be most financially beneficial to the manager.

Option 1:
- Hourly base of $9.00 annually bringing the position to $17,280.00. This is based on full-time employment.
- Paid vacation. One week after 2 years service and two weeks after 5 years service.
- Health insurance. 50/50 pay after 90 days.

PRODUCT STRATEGY

Current Product
Proprietary information is available to investors upon signature of a Non-Disclosure Agreement.

What sets Barber & Style College, Inc. apart from the competition is the combination of training students to perform services on men and women. Barber & Style College also is the only private school in the Florida Area. Barber & Style College will be the most technologically advanced barber styling school establishment in Florida. I believe with the funding changes with vocational education, you will see more advanced academics forming.
XYZ is a product well-known in Florida. It is used by many salons. This is not a threat; however, it is support for the school and for retail. We have the largest inventory of any salon. Our goal is to produce 35% in retail. This is a conservative number. Offering a singular note to product lines provides manageable inventory control XYZ also compliments our technological position, having a website that provides advertising and referrals. Presently, we are having a website designed for Barber & Style College. Here retailing will expand along with consultation services.

For their education center, XYZ offers 40% discounts on all professional sizes. This complements clinic pricing, keeping overhead down. At the Vocational Training Center, I used XYZ and the clinic retailed an average of 32%. The average salon retails 25%. Automation is key for inventory control.

The services offered include:

- Haircuts, color, hand, and nail treatments and XYZ products. This is a product line designed for men and women. The price point is average. $7 haircuts.

- Barber & Style- Hair design, colorization, chemical reconstruction, scalp massage and reconstruction, natural and alternative nail treatments, makeup (lessons and application, facials and, waxing).
- Barber & Style College -1500-hour barber styling course, a 750 hour course for cosmetology to barber styling, a 340-barber technician course, a 450-hour instructors' course. Of course, there will be a clinic of barber styling offered to the public. There are discounted services performed by students. Retail will also enhance the operation.

Consumers want a quality service for an economical price. Barber & Style College has designed the business to meet this current trend. Today's students want a vocation that they can make them money. Consumers want money, time, and stress levels under control. We provide this.

MARKET ANALYSIS

Market Definition
According to the Occupational Outlook Quarterly, published by the U.S. Department of Labor, it shows the hair industry as a steadily growing occupation in the U.S. through 20XX. However, the Department of Labor also shows Nail Technicians as one of the 11 fastest growing occupations in the U.S. and barber styling as number 37 in the top 100 occupations. This is because Baby Boomers are youth oriented and will be the driving force for our industry for the next 20 years. Generation X is the target we are going after but the Baby Boomers will be paying the way. Wellness, relaxation, and nurturing the soul will supersede "beauty services."

Barber & Styling is as large an industry as the tobacco industry. Big businesses are recognizing the billions of dollars consumers spend each year in our industry and they are buying up the major manufactures. Redken was bought by Cosimar, Matrix by Proctor and Gamble to use as two examples.

Locally, consumers demand pampering treatments while on vacation. Today's stress-relieving treatments replace the 20XX's party scene and corporate rewards are given with "Day of Beauty" packages.

The overall market demands quality service at a fair price.

Future Opportunities
As our client base builds in the local market, targeting marketing to the high school students and adults wanting a career change will bring new opportunities. Many high school students are attending vocation schools instead of four year colleges.

Customer Profile
Our primary customers are our students between the ages of 18 and 35 years of age. Our secondary customers are our walk in clients. Automation plays an important role in tracking clients, finding out which marketing areas are returning an investment, which the client is, and what their spending habits are. This is a continuous process.

Competition
The three top hair schools in Florida are Paul Mitchell, Aveda Beauty Academy and Jon Blue Beauty. They target only Baby Boomers and are high end quality cosmetology schools all competing for the same clients. None target male clients or teach male hair cutting and shaving. Our vocational training school will market to high school students and adults.

Risk
James and I could die before the business has established its systems.

Planned financing may not be met in the timeframe we would like. This would postpone the school.

Addressing risks is part of our regular planning. The better the plan, the less the risk, but they need to be addressed continually.

Marketing Plan

The marketing plans are presently in the development stages. Barber & Style College is playing an important role in this area of business. Strategy can be defined as the science of planning and directing large-scale operations, specifically of maneuvering forces into the most advantageous position prior to taking action. It is this area of business I enjoy the most. It is creative and easily measured. More time is needed for proper planning. We have already budgeted this area to 3% of total revenue.

On January 24, 20XX, Barber & Style College will be mapping out a 12-month promotional grid. In the next two weeks the logo should be complete and ready for copy. The storefront design will soon be finalized. Press releases will be sent out March 1. Direct marketing will introduce the now enrolling students and new service and product menus. Recruitment for the school will be done quarterly. Employees will involve themselves in the community.

All of this will be developed, mapped out, and evaluated.

Measurable results include:

- increased sales
- increased market share
- improved image
- increased knowledge of business
- identified competitive advantage
- created improved climate for future sales

When completed, it will be the best for the industry in this area and it will safely grow the business 10% annually. Although in the past, I have experienced up to 30% in a year. 10% is conservative and steady.

Market Environment

"With high-tech there must be high touch," says John Nesbitt, *Mega Trends 20XX*. Our society is stressed out and barber styling schools are convenient retreats. A relaxing environment, with customer service providing preventative services and products at a good price. Many women enjoy a relaxing facial for skin maintenance benefits; however, with an average household income of $26,949.00, it is a luxury. Now market the same service, networking facial with a purchase of $50.00 in cosmetics, and you have an affordable value-added service. Many men enjoy a relaxing shave and haircut. Marketing is key. Know the clients, their habits, likes, and dislikes. To do this, the school must be automated.

FINANCIALS

Profit and Loss Projections for the First 12 Months

Gross Tuition	$1,100,000	Based on 100 students at $11,000 each
Gross Services	$ 100,000	Based on clinic services of $2,000 per wk
Gross Retail	$ 125,000	Based on products, kits, vending machines

Gross Revenue   **$1,325,000**

OPERATING EXPENSES

Employees	$240,000
Rent	$ 48,000
Supplies	$ 60,000
Marketing	$ 24,000
Lights	$ 12,000
Accountant	$ 8,000
Financial Aid Servicer	$ 6,000
Accreditation	$ 4,000
Phone	$ 3,000
Copy Machine	$ 3,000
Janitor	$ 2,000
Gas	$ 1,800
Postage	$ 1,800
Paychex Company	$ 1,200
Water	$ 1,200
Insurance	$ 1,000
Waste Service	$ 1,000
Credit Card Machine	$ 600
Internet Service	$ 600
Alarm	$ 360
Total Operating Expenses	**$419,560**
Net Income	**$905,440**

Amortization Schedule

Principal: 260,000
Term: 60 Payments
Annual Interest Rate: 9.500
Payments Per Year: 12
Monthly Payment Amount: 5,460.48

Start-Up Costs

Purchase of Business	$100,000
School Equipment	$35,000
Classroom Equipment	$ 6,000
Office Equipment	$11,000
Plumbing	$ 3,000
Electrical	$ 4,000
Structural Needs	$ 7,000
Sign	$ 3,000
Phone Expenses	$ 3,200
License	$ 600
Printing	$ 1,000
Advertising	$ 5,000
Retail Inventory	$ 1,500
	$180,300
6 months Rent In Savings	$ 24,000
	$204,300
Loan	**$260,000**
Cash on hand	**$55,700**

How this will be paid back

1. Refer to amortization for loan payment. 5 year return on investment.
2. Refer to financial statements following.
3. Refer to projected income based on school productivity. In reality a school should graduate 100 students per year. This is realistic in theory and application. Worst case, the school graduates only **50** students in a year. These projections are based on a worst case scenario. The school will still have $331,240 left after expenses to pay on the loan.

FINANCIALS
Profit and Loss Projections for the First 12 Months

Gross Tuition	$550,000	Based on 50 students at $11,000 each
Gross Services	$ 50,000	Based on clinic services of $1,000 per wk
Gross Retail	$ 75,000	Based on products, kits, vending machines

Gross Revenue   **$675,000**

OPERATING EXPENSES
Employees	$180,000
Rent	$ 48,000
Supplies	$ 45,000
Marketing	$ 24,000
Lights	$ 12,000
Accountant	$ 8,000
Financial Aid Servicer	$ 6,000
Accreditation	$ 4,000
Phone	$ 3,000
Copy Machine	$ 3,000
Janitor	$ 2,000
Gas	$ 1,800
Postage	$ 1,000
Paychex Company	$ 1,200
Water	$ 1,200
Insurance	$ 1,000
Waste Service	$ 1,000
Credit Card Machine	$ 600
Internet Service	$ 600
Alarm	$ 360

Total Operating Expenses   **$343,760**
Net Income   **$331,240**

Worst/Worst case, the school graduates only **25** students in a year. These projections are based on a worst/worst case scenario. The school will still have $104,240 left after expenses to pay on the loan.

FINANCIALS
Profit and Loss Projections for the First 12 Months

Gross Tuition	$275,000	Based on 25 students at $11,000 each
Gross Services	$ 25,000	Based on clinic services of $500 per wk
Gross Retail	$ 50,000	Based on products, kits, vending machines

Gross Revenue $350,000

OPERATING EXPENSES
Employees	$100,000
Rent	$ 48,000
Supplies	$ 30,000
Marketing	$ 24,000
Lights	$ 10,000
Accountant	$ 8,000
Financial Aid Servicer	$ 6,000
Accreditation	$ 4,000
Phone	$ 3,000
Copy Machine	$ 3,000
Janitor	$ 2,000
Gas	$ 1,800
Postage	$ 800
Paychex Company	$ 800
Water	$ 800
Insurance	$ 1,000
Waste Service	$ 1,000
Credit Card Machine	$ 600
Internet Service	$ 600

Alarm		$ 360

Total Operating Expenses $245,760
Net Income $104,240

This means running the school five days a week.

School hours are Tuesday thru Friday 9am to 8pm and Saturday 8am to 6pm.

Total productive hours   54 hours per week
(Operating with **100** students per year)

		Breakeven To Pay Expenses
$1,325,000	year	$419,560.00
$110,041.66	month	$ 34,963.33
$27,604.17	week	$ 8,740.83
$5,520.83	day	$ 1,748.16
$102	hour	$ 32.37

This means running the school five days a week.

School hours are Tuesday thru Friday 9am to 8pm and Saturday 8am to 6pm.

Total productive hours   54 hours per week
(Operating with **50** students per year)

		Breakeven To Pay Expenses
$675,000	year	$343,760.00
$56,250	month	$ 28,646.66
$14,062.50	week	$ 7,161.66
$2,812.50	day	$ 1,432.33
$52	hour	$ 26.52

This means running the school five days a week.

School hours are Tuesday thru Friday 9am to 8pm and Saturday 8am to 6pm.

Total productive hours   54 hours per week
(Operating with **25** students per year)

		Breakeven To Pay Expenses
$350,000	year	$245,760.00
$29,166.67	month	$ 20,480.00
$7,291.66	week	$ 5,120.00
$1,458.33	day	$ 1,024.00
$27	hour	$ 18.96

Profit and Loss Projections for Five Months

Gross Tuition	$1,100,000	(Based on 100 students at $11,000 each)
Gross Services	$ 100,000	(Based on clinic services of $2,000 per wk)
Gross Retail	$ 125,000	(Based on products, kits, vending machines)

Gross Revenue for   **$552,208**

OPERATING EXPENSES

Employees	$100,000
Rent	$ 20,000
Supplies	$ 25,000
Marketing	$ 10,000
Lights	$ 5,000
Accountant	$ 3,333
Financial Aid Servicer	$ 2,500
Accreditation	$ 4,000
Phone	$ 1,667
Copy Machine	$ 1,250
Janitor	$ 833
Gas	$ 750
Postage	$ 750
Paychex Company	$ 500
Water	$ 500
Insurance	$ 416
Waste Service	$ 416
Credit Card Machine	$ 250
Internet Service	$ 250
Alarm	$ 150
Total Operating Expenses	**$177,565**
Net Income	**$374,643**

CHAPTER 14

BOOTH RENTAL CONTRACT

<u>Studio Hair Gallery</u>

Independent Contractor Agreement

**4015 Clarksville Hwy Suite A
Nashville, TN 37218
(615) XXX-XXXX**

This Independent Contractor (Hair Stylist) agreement is made effective this date_____; by and between the following parties:_____
_____and Studio Hair Gallery identified from here on out as The Company.

This Independent Contractor agreement is contracted for the sole purpose of enabling the said Independent, _____
_____

to render professional Hair services at the <u>Studio Hair Gallery</u> located at 4015 Clarksville Hwy: solely as an Independent Contractor.

As an Independent Contractor, you are responsible for rendering the aforementioned services, following the subsequent specifications and guidelines discussed herein:

1. ENGAGEMENT

The Independent Contractor/Commission Stylist accepts an engagement to provide the company <u>Studio Hair Gallery</u> with Hair Services.

2. TERM

_____, said Independent Contractor, shall provide services within the confines of the company, <u>Studio Hair Gallery</u>, during this agreement beginning on ___ _____ and ending on___

Independent Contractor must give a 30 day notice before leaving.

3. PARKING AREA

Said independent, _____, shall be responsible for parking vehicles on the side of building in the designated area.

4. AVAILABILITY FOR WORK

The daily schedule and work hours worked under this Agreement on a given day shall generally be subject to the Independent Contractors discretion.

5. COMPENSATION

Option #1 Said Independent,_____ shall pay <u>Studio Hair Gallery,</u> $<u>125.00</u> , per week for the usage of the Company facility for the purpose of servicing hair. Payment of each week is due by 6:00pm each Saturday.

March 1, 2XXX booth rent will only go up to $25.00 more. Late fee of $5.00 will be added daily for Independent Contractors, who pay after 6:00pm Saturday.

6. CONVENANT NOT TO COMPETE

During the term of this Agreement and for a period of twelve (12) months hereafter, the Independent Contractor/ shall not within a five(5) mile radius, directly or indirectly provide services to another business other than Studio Hair Gallery. Independent Contractor can, however work with another organization outside that five (5) mile radius.

7. ROLE OF THE INDEPENDENT CONTRACTOR

A) The Independent Contractor is and throughout this Agreement shall be an Independent Contractor, the said Independent, is not an employee, partner, or agent of the aforementioned Company.

B) The Independent Contractor shall not be entitled to, nor receive any benefits, such as, vacation pay, sick leave, retirement, or health care. Booth rent is due regardless if you do not work.

C) The Company shall not be responsible for withholding income and/or other taxes.

D) The Independent Contractor shall be solely responsible for filing all returns and paying any income, social security, or other taxes.

E) Furthermore, the Independent Contractor will provide copies of all documentation illustrating that said Independent

Independent Contractor has legally obtained the following:

aa.) Relevant Licenses
bb.) Internal Revenue Documentation
cc.) Met All State City Requirements

These items should include, but not limited to: Federal, State, and City Business Requirements, Employment Identification

Number, Business Name Registration, and unemployment Compensation Tax Numbers.

8. TOOLS AND SUPPLIES

The Independent Contractor shall be solely responsible for tools and supplies necessary or appropriate for the performance of the said Independent's services rendered hereunder.

9. INSURANCE COVERAGE

The Company will not be responsible for any fines, penalties or other costs incurred due to the actions, services rendered, or negligence of the Independent Contractor.

It is the sole responsibility of the Independent Contractor to obtain the necessary insurance to cover their business activities, including malpractice insurance, with the City Law of Nashville and the State Law of Tennessee.

10. PHONE USAGE

Each independent contractor can have their own personal phone line in their own name or they can use the company phone.

11. ASSURANCE DEPOSIT

To secure a work area or booth to render services, a deposit of $XX is due to the Company upon the signing of this Agreement.

Upon termination of this Agreement the said deposit will be fully returned to the said Independent, provided that the designated access area(s) is returned to the Company in the same condition in which it was received, to a reasonable extent.

12. DAMAGES

If any items are missing or damaged, the said Independent Contractor will be held responsible, and hereby agrees to replace or reimburse the said items to the Company at the full cost of replacement, including freight.

13. INSPECTIONS

The Company reserves the right to inspect any areas of the facility and packages coming in and out of the facility any time with reasonable cause.

All Independent Contractor must abide by state laws, regulations, and polices regarding safety, sanitation, and salon up keep. Furthermore, NO alcoholic beverages, drugs, firearms, weapons, or gambling are allowed on the premises of the Company. Any Independent Contractor caught violating the aforementioned guidelines in any way constitutes the Company the right to annul any agreement and the right to immediate termination on this Agreement.

14. UNACCEPTABLE BEHAVIOR

By accepting the terms outlined in this Agreement with this Company, the said Independent has a responsibility to the Company and his/her fellow colleagues in the facility to adhere to the Company's guidelines on behavior and conduct.
The purpose of these guidelines is not to restrict the personal freedoms of the said Independent, but rather to create and maintain an agreeable atmosphere for all individuals, for both those employed and those not employed through the Company.

Any Independent Contractor caught violating guidelines in any way, will constitute an automatic termination of this agreement.

15. ADVERTISEMENT

All Independent Contractor is responsible for their own advertisement.

16. MANAGEMENT DUTY'S

Each Independent Contractor is their own boss.

17. HOUSEKEEPING

The said Independent Contractor is expected to keep their designated areas neat and orderly at all times; it is a required safety precaution, to maintain high sanitation standards at all times. This Agreement may be terminated or annulled by the Independent Contractor for the following:

A) Breach or default of any material obligation of the Company, which is not cured within five (5) days of written notice

B) Organization hiring of any unlicensed person

C) If the Company files protection under the federal bankruptcy laws, or close their doors or have their business terminated as a result of the Company with non-professional or unlicensed persons.

THIS AGREEMENT CONSTITUTES THE FINAL UNDERSTANDING AND AGREEMENT BETWEEN THE PARTIES WITH RESPECT TO THE SUBJECT MATTER HEREIN, AND SUPERSEDES ALL PRIOR NEGOTIATIONS, UNDERSTANDINGS, AND AGREEMENTS BETWEEN THE PARTIES, WHETHER WRITTEN OR ORAL. THIS AGREEMENT MAY, HOWEVER, BE AMMENDED, SUPPLEMENTED, OR CHANGED ONLY BY AN AGREEMENT

SIGNED BY BOTH PARTIES.

IN WITNESS THEREOF, this Agreement has been excused by the parties as of the date first written above and signed below.

The Independent Contractor
"Said Independent"

_____
(Independent's Signed Name)

_____
(Independent's Printed Name)

_____
(mm/dd/yy)

The Company/Authorized Agent

_____
(Company Rep Signature)

_____
(Company Re Printed Name)

_____
(mm/dd/yy)

CHAPTER 15

THINGS I LEARNED FROM MY MENTOR
"WORKING ON YOUR BUSINESS, NOT IN IT"

Your Barber Styling Business and your life are two totally separate things. Your business is something apart from you, rather than a part of you. Once you recognize that the purpose of your life is not to serve your business, but that the primary purpose of your business is to serve your life, you can then go to work on your business, rather than in it.

Pretend that the Barber Styling Business you own or want to own is the prototype for 1,000 more just like it. That your business is going to serve as the model for 1,000 more exactly like it. All perfect clones.

Now understand the rules of the Business Model:

*The model will provide consistent value to your customer, employees, suppliers, and lenders, beyond what they expect.
*The model will be operated by people with the lowest possible level of skill.
*The model will stand out as a place of impeccable order.
*All work in the model will be documented in Operations Manuals.
*The model will provide a uniformly predictable service to the customer.
*The model will utilize a uniform color, dress and facilities code.

Let's take a look at each of these rules.

The model will provide consistent value to your customer, employees, suppliers, and lenders, beyond what they expect.

What is value? How do we understand it. Value is what people perceive it to be. What can your business do to provide consistent value to your customers, employees, suppliers, and lenders but would provide it beyond their expectations. Value can be your products, service or a simple word of thanks.

The model will be operated by people with the lowest possible level of skill.

If your model depends on highly skilled people, it's going to be impossible to duplicate. Highly skilled people are very expensive which means you will have to raise the price of your product or service. You need to create the very best system through which good people can be leveraged to produce great results.

The question you need to ask yourself is how can I give my customer the results he wants systematically rather than personally?

How can you create an expert system rather than hiring an expert?

Great businesses are built by ordinary people doing extraordinary things. For ordinary people to do extraordinary things, a system , which is a way of doing things, is required in order to compensate for the skills your people have and the skills your business needs if it is going to produce constant and consistent results.

The system is the tools your people use to increase their productivity, to get the job done in the way it needs to get done in order for your business to successfully be different from your competition. It's our job to teach your people how to use the system. Ordinary People can make your job much easier. Most owners of a small business prefer highly skilled people because he believes they make his job easier and he can just leave them to run his business. Unfortunately the result of this kind of thinking is based on how the people feel who are running the business. If the people are not in a good mood or having problems at home the business will suffer. If they are in a good mood the business does good. In this kind of business, a business that relies on discretion, "How do I motivate my people becomes the constant question?" "How do I keep them in the mood." It is literally impossible to produce a consistent result in a business that depends on extraordinary people. No business can do it for long. And no extraordinary business tries to!

Because every extraordinary business knows that when you intentionally build your business around the skills of ordinary people, you will be forced to ask the question about how to produce a result without the extraordinary people.

You will be forced to find a system that leverages your ordinary people to the point where they can produce extraordinary results over and over again. You will be forced to build a business that works.

The model will stand out as a place of impeccable order.

People crave order although we live in a world of disorder. Individuals need structure in their life. A life lacking in comprehensive structure is a life heading for a wreck. A business that looks orderly says to your customer that your people know what they're doing. A business that looks orderly says to your customer that he can trust in the result. A business that looks orderly says that the structure is in place.

All work in the model will be documented in Operations Manuals.

Documentation beats Conversation. Documentation says, "This is how we do it." Documentation provides your people with the structure they need and with a written account of how to get the job done in the most efficient and effective way. Documentation is an affirmation of order. By making clear demands on their time and energy, it provides structure around which the rest of their lives can be organized.

The Operations Manual is the businesses How To Do It Guide. It has the steps needed to do, the purpose of the work and shows how to achieve the desired results.

The model will provide a uniformly predictable service to the customer.

The business should look orderly and it should act orderly. It must do things in predictable and uniform way.

This is the experience that most people have with Barber Stylist.

I went to a barbershop and in my first meeting, the Barber Stylist gave me one of the best fades I had ever had. He was a Master Barber. He used the electric clippers the entire time and never used the shears. He gave me a great shampoo before he cut my hair. During the haircut his assistant gave me fresh coffee. The experience was very enjoyable, so I made another appointment for two weeks later.

When I returned two weeks later my whole experience was different. The Barber Stylist used the shears about fifty percent of the time. He did not shampoo my hair before cutting it, nor did he even show me the mirror and ask how I wanted it cut. The assistant did not even offer me a cup of coffee, because they were too busy folding towels. The fade was perfectly blended and my razor line was perfect. I was very pleased with my haircut.

As I left and got in my car, something in me decided not to go back for another appointment. It certainly was not the haircut, he did an excellent job. It was not the barber, he was nice and pleasant. I thought about why I was not going back to the shop.

There was no consistency to the experience. The expectations created at the first appointment were never the same. I was not sure what to expect. The unpredictability said nothing about the barber, other than that he was constantly changing my experience for me. He was in control of my experience, not I. He was running the business for him, not for me.

I didn't matter what I wanted.

It didn't matter that I enjoyed the sound of the clippers and shears, also the hot lather with the razor.

It didn't matter that I enjoyed being waited on by his assistant to bring me fresh coffee.

It didn't matter that I enjoyed the experience of having a shampoo before I had my haircut.

The Barber Stylist gave me a perfect experience and then he took it away. It is like the "Burnt Child Syndrome". This is where the child is punished and rewarded for the same kind of behavior. This form of behavior in a parent can be disastrous to the child; he never knows what to expect or how to act. The Burnt Child has no choice but to stay with the parent. But the Burnt Customer can go to another shop and he will.

Make sure you do the same thing the same way every time.

The model will utilize a uniform color, dress and facilities code.

Marketing studies tell us that all consumers are moved to act by colors and shapes they find in the business. Believe it or not, the colors, smells and shapes of your model can make or break your business! The shape of your sign, your logo, the type styles used on your business cards will have a significant impact on your business.

Let's summarize what we have covered so far.

Go to work on your business rather in it.

Go to work on your business as if 1,000 others will use the same prototype.

Think of your business as something apart from yourself, as a world of its own.

Think of your business as anything but a job.

Ask yourself the following questions:

How can I get my business to work without me?

How can I get my people to work without me constantly coaching them on what to do?

How can I create a system for my business in such a

way that it could be duplicated 1,000 times, so the $1,000^{th}$ unit would run as smoothly as the first?

How can I own my business and still be free of it?

How can I spend my time doing the work I love to do rather than the work I have to do?

If you are a Barber Stylist and asked yourself these questions, you'll eventually tell yourself that you don't have the answers. That has been the problem for so many Barber Stylist.

Things will be different, because now you know what you don't know. Now you are ready to look the problem in the eye.

The problem isn't your business, it is You. It has always been you and will always be you, until you change.

Until you change your view about what a business is and how it works.

Until you begin to think about your business in a totally new way.

Until you accept the fact that a business must be run by a proven system and model.

To successfully develop a great business model and system, just follow a proven model, go to a training seminar and implement the same proven system in your Barber Styling School or Salon. A proven way to the top that has been successfully implemented by thousands of Barber Stylist just like you.

We call it "How To Run A Million Dollar School Seminar.

To find out more about How To Run A Million Dollar School Seminar, read the next chapter.

CHAPTER 16

HOW TO RUN A MILLION DOLLAR SCHOOL SEMINAR

If you try to learn how to swim by watching dvd's and reading books on swimming - you will drown in the water. A wise person will always attend a hands on training class by a proven master!

So, what exactly is "How To Run A Million Dollar School Seminar"?

The Seminar is a 2 day live training program that shows you, step-by-step, how to build a unique and profitable Barber & Styling School, become accredited, receive government grants, market more effectively and turn your school into a 24/7 money-making, world-changing school. We're honored to have many outstanding reviews from our graduates.

Learning made easy. TELL, SHOW & DO!
Our goal is to make your learning experience as easy and enjoyable as possible.
That's why every module is delivered in a hands on environment and multimedia format. Learn from your computer and enjoy our hands on training classroom setting. "You get behind the wheel and actually operate the school".
You can't learn how to swim by watching videos and reading books on swimming, you must take a live hands on training workshop to learn how to swim!

The Seminar Curriculum & Schedule
The core Seminar curriculum is focused on the five pillars of growing a million dollar school business. The program is

2 days long and includes full hands on training. Pick your two consecutive days of training.

See exactly what's in each module.
- *PROFIT PLAN*
- *BUSINESS PLAN*
- *ACCREDITITAION*
- *FINANCIAL AID SCHOOL*
- *AUTOMATION SYSTEM*

MODULES: SET A SOLID FOUNDATION FOR YOUR LONG-TERM SUCCESS
Profit Clarity

*How to run a multi-million dollar school (hands on training)
*State Board Rules & Regulations for a school
*How to identify and create your schools lucrative profit streams
*How to get a crystal clear picture of how your school makes money so that you can finally stop wasting time on unprofitable income streams

Creating Your School Business Plan
*How to assess and reduce risk of the school
*How to calculate how much money will you need to start
*The top failure factors verses success factors of schools
*Checklist for: Lease, location and equipment
*What are all the staffing responsibilities
*Marketing Plan
* How to calculate how much money your school will profit

Steps To Accreditation
*Schedule of fees for accreditation
*Application for accreditation
*Admissions policy and procedures: enrollment agreement requirements and checklist
*Catalog requirements and checklist

*Evaluation of students: satisfactory academic progress policy and checklist and checklist
*Financial practices and management: withdrawal and settlement policy
*Student, faculty and administrative interview guide
*Onsite inspection visit for accreditation
Tips and secrets from experience of school accreditation inspections

Financial Aid Process
*New School financial aid guide for your school to follow
*How to properly fill out a financial aid application
*How to know if a student is eligible for financial aid
*How your school can be eligible to receive financial aid
*How to calculate how much financial aid a student will receive
*How to process and manage the millions of dollars of financial aid

School Automation System
*You get behind the wheel and actually run the school
*Master the ultimate school software system in 3 easy steps
*How to easily track student hours
*How to easily track financial aid
*How to easily teach students theory and give test
*How to keep student records perfect
*How to pass every school audit

Plus, I'll be there to help you along the way.
We've set up dynamic support structures throughout the program to help you implement, take massive action and get results.

Live "Office Hours" Calls Every Week
We'll be by your side every step of the way. Not sure how a specific idea applies? Need help? We can help. We'll answer

your questions live on the calls, plus you'll be able to submit questions in advance and we'll answer them.

Two Full Implementation Hands On Training Days

We know you're crazy busy. That's why we've built in two full consecutive days that you can choose anytime of the week.

The Answer Vault
Each and every module in the Workshop is robust and sparks new ideas, and new questions. You'll keep access to us, so you'll always have precise wisdom at your fingertips.

Your Workshop Investment
It's important that you know the full value you'll get in this workshop. These values are not inflated nor created out of thin air. They are honest, good faith estimate since you cannot attend any class with this information in one setting.

The Core Five Pillars Training: This five unit system has taken us years and hundreds of thousands of dollars to learn, distill, refine, and package for you in an easy-to-follow format that gets results. This includes live one on one training, transcripts, action guides and manuals. **($10,000 Value)**

Bonus Done-For-You Word Document Files, Checklist & Contracts: If you've ever hired a business consultant to create done-for-you materials, or spent hours looking for the right resources, then you know how valuable this is. **($3,000 Value)**

Weekly "Office Hours": Ask us questions, get feedback and more. Private coaching within our previous Adventure Mastermind program cost $12,000 per year.
($7,000 Value)

Total Workshop Value $20,000

Total Seminar Investment Only $1,999
For more info, email: 1chin@comcast.net or
visit www.millionairebarberstylist.com

Proof about "How To Run A Million Dollar School Seminar"

The Seminar is a proven program that gets results. Read previous workshop attendee reviews.

Arlo Washington- **Owner of Washington Barber College 501-568-8800**

"Mrs. Velma and Uchendi empowered and equipped me to open my own Barber College, get accredited and receive financial aid. The two day class had priceless information. I am a former barber that dreamed of going to the next level. I always wanted my own school, so I could give back and of course make more money without working behind the chair 12 hours each day. It was well worth it. I got to learn the info that Millionaire's know, but I got to live like a Millionaire for those two days. My school is now accredited and we receive financial aid. The two day class is for any Barber or Stylist that wants to achieve their dreams.

Lois Bryant-Owner of Pyramid Beauty and Barber School 901-276-5325

I just want to say how much I loved the experience. I received the Presidential Experience. They took me to the Multi-Million Dollar Barber Styling School and I learned so much information about business. It was a 3 step learning process: TELL, SHOW & DO! I left with more information than I expected.

David Hiland- Two Time World Barber Battle Champion *winfreysbarber@gmail.com*

"This class is for all Barbers that just work behind a chair each day or run a shop. I just wanted to thank Mrs. Velma and Uchendi for all your business help. You were so kind and patient and creative and insightful. I totally felt spoiled,
You rolled out the red carpet treatment. Thank you for the business manuals on Starting, Running & Growing a Barber School. I enjoyed the hands on training. I learn better when it is hands on. I learned a lot about the business of how it operates by following a system. I was growing tired of working behind the chair each day and wanted to move on up and become a successful business owner. Thank you for the booth rental contracts, the blue print on becoming accredited and the blue print on operating a school.

Kumasi Barefield-Owner of Networks Barber College 708-868-8115

"I loved working with Mrs. Velma and Uchendi because they are very honest and very down to earth people. It was an experience of a life time to be able to learn first hand from someone who could identify with me. My school is now accredited by NACCAS and we are receiving financial aid. My enrollment has tripled. I love the one on one calls, where I can just pick up the phone and call them when I have questions.

Then we got down to business. They took me to the Multi-Million Dollar Barber Styling School and I learned so much, because I got to actually run the school with hands on training. I really needed that type of training. I am a hands on learner. I recommend this class for all Barbers & Stylists who want to make lots of money and help people.

Uchendi "Chin" Nwani Is Available For Keynote Speeches.

He delivers keynote addresses to many private and public organizations, schools, corporations, churches and prisons. Each year he addresses thousands of people.
Uchendi presents inspiring, motivating and informative talks for many audiences. His motivating talks have brought immediate changes and long lasting results. To find out how Uchendi can change the life of your organization, log onto www.millionairebarberstylist.com or email 1chin@comcast.net

For The Seminar or Speaking Engagements
Email: 1chin@comcast.net or log onto
www.millionairebarberstylist.com

YES, send ___ copies of The Millionaire Barber Stylist

Complete and mail this order form with payment to:
International Barber & Style College
3744 Annex Avenue Suite A 2
Nashville, TN 37209
Phone: 1-615-354-0166
E-mail: 1chin@comcast.net
Web Site: www.millionairebarberstylist.com

- ___ Copies of The Millionaire Barber Stylist…$19.99 each
- ___ Copies of The Millionaire Ex-Convict…$19.99 each
- ___ Shipping and Handling $3.50 for first book, and $1.50 for each additional book
- ___ Shipping and Handling $3.50
- ___ Volume I & II Clipper Cutting New Millennium Fade DVD $59.99
- ___ Overnight express available for $18.00 extra

$_____ TOTAL ENCLOSED

RUSH TO:
Name:_____

Address_____

City_____State_____Zip_____

Phone # _____

Order by check, money order, VISA, MasterCardCredit

Card Type:_____

Credit Card Number:_____ Exp:_____

Signature_____

365

taylor. Quenita Vahoulon